SLA GUIDELINES

Priority Paperwork

Policy Making and Development Planning for Primary and Secondary School Libraries

Rachel Sargeant

Series Editor: Geoff Dubber

Acknowledgements

Rachel Sargeant would like to acknowledge Pat Lipinski of Gloucestershire Library Services for Education, and Geoff Dubber and Jane Cooper of the SLA for their help in providing academic and government sources for her research. She would also like to thank Nigel Sargeant for proofreading her early drafts.

Geoff Dubber and the SLA Publications Team would like to thank Rachel Sargeant for her time and expertise in turning what started out as a primary school publication to one that addresses policy making and development across the primary and secondary age ranges. Thank you Rachel.

Geoff Dubber would also like to thank the other five busy librarian colleagues and friends for sharing their expertise and their paperwork, namely, Heather Bignold, Librarian at Clayesmore Prep School; Sally Dring, Librarian and Literacy and Numeracy Coordinator at Ripon Grammar School, long serving chair of the SLA's Yorkshire and Humberside branch and also a member of the SLA Board; Amy McKay, Librarian at Corby Business Academy, SLA School Librarian of the Year 2016 and currently a member of the SLA Board; Alison Tarrant, Director of the SLA, previously librarian at Cambourne Village College and SLA School Librarian of the Year Honour List 2017; Anne Thompson, Librarian at Notre Dame Prep School Cobham.

Published by

School Library Association
1 Pine Court, Kembrey Park
Swindon SN2 8AD

Tel: 01793 530166   Fax: 01793 481182
E-mail: info@sla.org.uk
Web: www.sla.org.uk

Registered Charity No: 313660
Charity Registered in Scotland No: SC039453

© School Library Association 2018. All rights reserved.
ISBN: 978-1-911222-17-0

Printed by Holywell Press, Oxford

Cover image: Pixabay/annca

SLA Guidelines: Priority Paperwork

Contents

Introduction	4
PART ONE: Library Policy	5
Purpose	5
How to write a Library Policy	7
Step 1: Define your aims	7
Step 2: Consider your services	7
Step 3: Write your first draft	9
Step 4: Consult widely about your draft document	15
Step 5: Publish your finished copy	16
Step 6: Promote your policy document	16
Step 7: Operate the Policy	17
Step 8: Update/Revise	17
PART TWO: Library Development Plan	18
Purpose	18
How to write a Library Development Plan	18
Step 1: Gather information and assess current situation	18
Step 2: Consult	20
Step 3: Produce a draft	20
Step 4: Seek agreement and submit final copy	21
Step 5: Implement the plan	21
Step 6: Review and Revise	21
PART THREE: Case studies and documentation	22
Appendix 1: Dean Close Preparatory School, Cheltenham Library Policies and Development Plan	22
Appendix 2: Notre Dame Preparatory School, Cobham Case Study and Library Policy	32
Appendix 3: Claysmore Preparatory School, Iwerne Minster, Dorset Library Policies	39
Appendix 4: Cambourne Village College, Cambridgeshire Case Study, Library Policy and Development Plan	45
Appendix 5. Corby Business Academy Library Development Plan	58
Appendix 6. Ripon Grammar School Library Policy and Development Plan	63
Bibliography	71

Introduction

School libraries are complex organisations with many moving parts. They exist to meet the needs of their school community at a time when school priorities, curricula and technology are evolving.

Whether in a primary or secondary school, and whether a small collection of books in a corridor or a multi-media learning resource centre, your library can have a significant impact on your school community. In their report into school libraries, the Libraries All Party Parliamentary Group cited much international research evidence on the impact of school libraries on pupil attainment, achievement and motivation. It is significant that they entitled their report: *The Beating Heart of the School.*[1]

But for the library to be an effective whole-school resource, it is essential to set out how it operates – its policies and procedures – and to have a clear plan for how the school intends to develop it in a given timescale. Hence the need to write a library policy and subsequently a library development plan.

This updated guide is based on two previous SLA publications – *Practical Paperwork: Policy Making and Development Planning for the Primary School Library* (2007) by Kay Harrison and Tricia Adams and *Paperwork Made Easy: Policy Making and Development Planning for the Secondary School Library* (2008) by Lynn Winkworth and Geoff Dubber.

This guide will:

- Explain how to draw up a Library Policy, explaining the process step by step
- Provide examples of actual policy documents from primary and secondary schools to show the theory of policy writing put into practice
- Explain how to draw up a Library Development Plan
- Provide examples of development plans which show different priorities, targets and formats
- Give suggestions for further reading for those keen to learn more about current school library thinking and best practice.

---

[1] All Party Parliamentary Group for Libraries (2014) *The Beating Heart of the School: Improving educational attainment through school libraries and librarians.* Viewed at https://www.cilip.org.uk/sites/default/files/documents/BeatingHeartoftheSchool.pdf [accessed 2/10/17]

SLA Guidelines: Priority Paperwork

PART ONE: Library Policy

What is a policy?

The Cambridge Online Dictionary defines a policy as:

> *a set of ideas or a plan of what to do in particular situations that has been agreed to officially by a group of people, a business organisation, a government, or a political party* [2]

A policy is a working document. The Library Policy is a summary of the school's current practices and a series of statements about how the school wants the library to be used.

The purpose of a policy

The International Federation of Library Associations and Institutions, the leading international body that represents the interests of those who rely on libraries and information professionals, states:

> *A school library should be managed within a clearly structured policy framework that recognises the library as a core resource and centre for reading and inquiry. A school library policy should be devised bearing in mind the overarching policies and needs of the school and should reflect the ethos, mission, aims and objectives, as well as the reality of the school.* [3]

The purpose of the library policy is to make clear to everyone in the school how the library should operate if it is to contribute successfully to pupil attainment. In particular, the policy could consider the following key questions:

- What is the purpose of our library?
- What help does it provide for staff in the delivery of the curriculum?
- How does it affect the quality of learning and learning styles?
- How does it contribute to a positive ethos and culture in the school?
- In what ways does it support and inspire pupils, including those with learning support needs and the gifted and talented?
- How does it promote the enjoyment of reading?
- How does it promote the development of lifelong skills for library use and information handling?
- How is it managed?
- What resources does it hold?
- How will it measure its success?

---

[2] http://dictionary.cambridge.org/dictionary/english/policy

[3] International Federation of Library Associations and Institutions (2015) *IFLA school library guidelines*, page 22. Viewed at https://www.ifla.org/files/assets/school-libraries-resource-centers/publications/ifla-school-library-guidelines.pdf [accessed 2/10/17]

Links to other school policies

A Library Policy document cannot stand in isolation. If it is to have credibility, it must reflect the thinking, practices and, ideally, the format of other policies in the school.

To refer to other school policies in its philosophy, in direct quotes and references, will give the library policy document strength and reinforce the library's central role in supporting the learning, teaching and daily routines of the whole school. It is sufficient to cross-reference other, relevant school policies rather than copying them in full into the Library Policy.

There are other school policy documents with which your library documentation can make supportive links.

Consider the following:

- Teaching and Learning
- Curriculum Policy
- Literacy and Numeracy
- ICT (including Acceptable Use Policy)
- Inclusion and Diversity policies
- Supervision of Children
- Safeguarding
- Behaviour Management
- School Budget
- Health and Safety
- Staff Development.

It is essential to read through these key policies and any others you think useful before you start your own.

Format

By constructing your document in the same style and format as others in your school, your policy will be seen as part of the corporate school documentation.

Your policy document will strengthen the school's view of your work and the ways in which the library contributes positively to learning and teaching.

Putting together a policy document can take weeks or even months, depending on its intended readership and the consultation processes it goes through.

Tone

It is best to adopt the tone of other policies written for your school. As your policy defines what the library is now, it should avoid use of the future tense and idealistic, visionary language. (What the library hopes to become needs to be dealt with incrementally in the Development Plan as explained later in the guide.) Unless the policy clearly explains current practices and thinking, the intended readership may not understand the current position. This can hinder library development.

Detail

Your document can be as detailed or as brief as you wish. Some alternatives are:

- A lengthy and in-depth text
- A one or two page sheet
- A summary sheet attached to a main policy document.

Length and detail will reflect your aim in writing, your intended readership, the complexity of the work of your school library, the manner in which you plan to promote the document and the way you expect others to use it. It can be one document or several. (For example, you may wish to create a separate stock selection policy, or overdue policy etc.)

Essentially, if you want it to be read and understood, it should be meaningful without being cumbersome. As previously mentioned, there is no need to duplicate other policies, simply reference them.

How to write a Library Policy

There are essentially 8 steps to policy writing:

- Define your aims/write your mission statement
- Consider your services
- Write/define what you do and how you do it under your chosen headings – this is your first draft copy
- Consult widely and redraft. Consult again
- Publish your finished copy
- Promote
- Operate
- Update/revise.

Step 1: Define your aims

The policy must reflect the general aims and objectives of the school and show how the library currently supports them.

The opening section of your policy document should be a clear list of aims or a mission statement. Ideally, it should link openly and clearly to the whole-school mission statement. This establishes the links between library policy and the whole school from the outset.

This opening section should help readers to understand the real purpose of the library. As a mission statement or series of aims, it illustrates why the school has invested staff, time, space and funding in the school library.

Step 2: Consider your services

Make a list of all the essential services that the library offers to its users across the school. These headings will provide the structure for your document.

Headings that you might consider include:

- Accommodation
- Access
- Resources
- Operating Procedures
- Staffing
- Library Use
- External Support
- Monitoring and Evaluation.

However, the choice of headings needs to reflect what is important to your library and your school. Below are the different headings used by four schools that provided their policy documents as case studies for the previous editions of this guide:

School A (Primary)
- Introduction
- Aims and Objectives
- Organisation
- Resources
- Monitoring and Review

School B (Primary)
- Introduction
- Aims
- Resources
- Environment
- Systems
- Information Literacy Skills
- How the Library will be promoted
- Monitoring

School C (Secondary)
- Mission Statement
- Objectives
- School Library Management and Communication
- Access
- Induction
- Code of Conduct
- Discipline
- Resources, Accommodation and Finance
- Monitoring and Evaluation

School D (Secondary)
- The School Library
- Ethos of Library
- Use of Library
- Resources Management
- Services

But remember to keep the document to a sensible length. Make it too detailed and no one will read it! If it's long and detailed consider adding an executive summary.

Step 3: Write your first draft

The arrangements and systems you have put in place to manage the library form the basis of your policy. Under your chosen headings, write down your existing practices/strategies as clearly as you understand them.

This can be challenging and will take time. You need to be honest but express everything in as positive a tone as possible. For example, current practice may require you to close the library during lesson times when you have other duties. This needs to be included in the policy document. By writing clear, concise and positive statements, the school should be able to see the importance of the library and any difficulties that are apparent. Policy writing will thus provide an opportunity for gaps to be identified and discussed, and for a range of new strategies to be included in the next Library Development Plan.

Remember that at this early stage, you are putting your perceptions on paper. It is not yet a whole-school policy document.

Useful Questions
The following questions may help you when considering what to write about your services.

But do not despair, if you have been asked to manage a library that is little more than a cupboard in the corridor. Simply use the questions that are currently relevant to you. Where the questions give you ideas for improvement, you could present some of these as targets in your Library Development Plan. (See Part Two of this guide.)

3.1 Accommodation
The location of the library as well as its environment, furniture and fittings are crucial in ensuring effective use.

- Is the library in a location where all classes, staff and pupils, can have easy access?
- Does the layout support the specific retrieval of information as well as opportunities for browsing and quiet reading?
- Is the shelving fit for purpose, able to display all types of resources and with clear guiding?
- Is the library comfortable and welcoming, with an atmosphere that is identifiably different from classrooms, yet conducive to learning?
- How are displays and library promotions organised and updated?
- Does the library have space to support information literacy through the integrated provision of digital resources, books and other learning resources?

SLA **Guidelines:** Priority Paperwork

3.2 Access
All staff in the school need to be clear on when the library is open, which classes can use it, and at what times individual pupils/students can visit it.

- What access do pupils and staff have to the library in terms of opening hours?
- How is the library timetabled for classes and what impact does this have on other users?
- Is access restricted because the library has a dual purpose, e.g. as a classroom or as an assumed (but perhaps unnamed) IT suite?
- Has any provision been made for pupils to visit the library before and after school, at break and lunchtimes?
- Is the library involved in any community use and/or out-of-hours learning activities? If so, how is this provision managed?

3.3 Learning resources
One of the key areas the library policy must address is the relationship between the library resources and other collections around the school:

- If there is fiction in the library, how does it relate to reading collections in the classrooms, English Department or Special Educational Needs Department (SEND)? How are these funded? Who manages them? How do staff and students understand the link between these collections?
- In a primary school – Are resources to support the delivery of the literacy strategy (e.g. reading scheme books) kept separately and if so, why and by whom?
- Are resources for teaching staff housed in the library, e.g. class sets, group readers, teaching manuals? (While the library should support the needs of the school community, thought must be given to storage versus display if pupils are to see the library as being for them.)
- In a primary school – Are all learning resources, including those held by subject co-ordinators, recorded on a library management system available in the library or through the school network?
- In a secondary school – to what extent are department resources recorded on the LMS and to what advantage to staff and students?

The policy should consider:

- What methods are used for selecting resources and what evaluation criteria are adopted?
- Who is responsible for selecting resources for the library and how do they involve other staff and pupils? How do they ensure impartiality in selection procedures?
- How are the current resources kept up to date, relevant and in good condition?
- Is the number of resources sufficient in quantity and range? (Make reference here to your annual spend per pupil.[4])

---

[4] The Booktrust worked with LISU at Loughborough University to arrive at a recommended spending figure per head on library books of £10 for primary and £14 for secondary. These figures, compiled in 2007, do not include set texts, textbooks or study guides. http://www.sla.org.uk/blg-school-libraries-booktrust-report-says.php [accessed 4/10/17]

- Does the school librarian/library coordinator undertake regular audits to assess stock gaps and devise shopping lists of priorities?
- Is there a variety of reading choices in the range of fiction genres and leisure interests to cater for all reading abilities and appetites?
- Does the school use Accelerated Reader? Which year groups participate in the scheme? When/how are supporting library lessons and online quizzing sessions timetabled? To what extent does this work support or detract from your reading for enjoyment strategies?
- How do library staff maintain awareness of new authors and areas of publishing?
- Does the range of resources reflect cultural diversity and support the school's inclusion and diversity policies?
- How is internet access managed and monitored? (Also refer here to your school's IT/Digital policy)
- Are teacher-recommended websites easily linked from the school intranet and available on terminals in the library?
- What provisions are there for magazines and newspapers, journals, DVDs, audio books, artefacts, etc.?
- Does the library operate an eBook loan service? How is this administered?
- Does the library lend eReaders, laptops, tablets? What are the procedures for borrowing? How does this benefit the pupils? Is it time effective for you?

3.4 Organisation

The library needs to be well organised if it is to meet its goals of allowing pupils to develop library skills and successfully retrieve information.

- How are the non-fiction books classified? For example, by the Dewey Decimal System, and perhaps by a simplified version for primary schools, with additional colour-coding if required?
- Does the classification system run in a logical order round the room and in correct numerical order from left to right within the bays?
- How are the fiction books organised? By genre? Or alphabetically by author's surname?

Pupils' ability to find what they are looking for will be greatly enhanced if there are visible search tools and shelf-guiding.

- Are the bays, shelves and sections clearly labelled with terms and phrases in familiar language? In secondary schools, label should preferably use the subject terminology taught in class.
- Do pupils have access to an online library catalogue?
- What mechanisms are available to help pupils find fiction genres and series they particularly like? How does this work with graphic novels which is often a challenge?
- In primary schools, how are the youngest pupils catered for? Subject indexes and shelf guiding could incorporate pictures or symbols for infants.

Straightforward borrowing procedures are essential if the library is to function successfully.

- What issuing system is used for lending resources? Is there a self-service system in operation?
- What management information does it provide?
- Are there clear routines for the return of books to the library and then to the shelves?
- How many books and other items can a pupil borrow and for how long?
- Do the staff use the issue system to borrow books for the classroom? What are their borrowing limits?
- Is there a facility for staff and pupils to request or reserve particular books?
- Does the library have a security system? What are the procedures for dealing with pupils (and staff) when the alarm is triggered?

For all but the smallest school libraries, an efficient computerised library management system will streamline administrative routines and provide useful monitoring data. The prime reason for its introduction will always be the impact on pupils' ability to search and retrieve information.

The library policy will need to consider:

- Who is creating the database to ensure consistency in key wording?
- Who has the ongoing responsibility for adding new books to the system as they are bought?
- How are loans recorded for books that are borrowed from the local Schools Library Service?
- Are library loans monitored and borrowing patterns used to inform literacy practices and future spending on books?

3.5 Management and Staffing

The management of the library, in terms of who is responsible and how it operates on a day-to-day basis, will have a major bearing on how effectively it contributes to teaching and learning.

The library policy should consider:

- Is there a member of the teaching staff with overall responsibility for the library? How much non-contact time is available for this?
- Has the school appointed a librarian or library assistant to work specifically in the library? If not, what steps are taken to ensure pupils' visits to the library are supported by an informed adult presence?
- What training is provided for those with library management responsibilities?
- Are library staff following CILIP's Ethical Principles and Code of Professional Practice? The Chartered Institute of Library and Information Professionals operates an Ethical Framework, covering such issues as confidentiality in dealing with library users, commitment to access to information and impartiality. It is highly recommended that all library staff follow the guidelines, whether CILIP members or not.[5]
- Does everyone with a library responsibility have a clear job description for their library role?

---

[5] CILIP Existing Ethical Framework (revised 2012) https://www.cilip.org.uk/research/topics/ethics-review/existing-ethical-framework [accessed 19/10/17]

3.6 Library Use and Curriculum Support

To assess the library's contribution to teaching and learning, consider how it contributes outside its four walls (if it has four walls!).

The policy could consider its impact on:

- classroom activity and lesson observation
- schemes of work and curriculum plans
- school self-evaluation form
- pupils' workbooks and displays
- discussion with pupils and teachers
- development plans and policies
- Public examination results.

These should all give an indication of how successfully the school is maximising its investment in the library. The real challenge for the library policy lies in getting it implemented and integrated across the whole curriculum, throughout the school.

There are two main aspects which should be considered.

3.6a Support for literacy and reading for pleasure

All pupils must be encouraged to read widely across both fiction and non-fiction to develop their knowledge of themselves and the world they live in, to establish an appreciation and love of reading, and to gain knowledge across the curriculum.[6]

Questions to consider are:

- Are pupils allowed to borrow books and in what numbers and take them home to read and enjoy?
- With younger children – Is the library used for story-times?
- Is the library used effectively for book and author promotion activities?
- Are pupils given opportunities to browse, select books from all categories of stock, and sit in the library and read?
- Are the skills and interests of teaching staff and departments across the school used in mounting displays and promoting interest in reading and information handling?
- Is the use of your public libraries services and neighbouring specialist libraries, archives etc. promoted by staff to pupils and encouraged among parents?
- Are pupils' reading choices monitored to provide evidence of literacy attainment and to inform book purchasing?
- How is the library used to promote new authors and widen pupils' reading diets?
- Does the school organise book weeks or author visits and how does the library contribute?

---

[6] Department for Education (2014) *National Curriculum in England: English programmes of study.* Viewed at https://www.gov.uk/government/publications/national-curriculum-in-england-english-programmes-of-study/national-curriculum-in-england-english-programmes-of-study [accessed 3/10/17]

- Does the library display pupils' book reviews and promote books and story recordings they have made themselves?
- Are there opportunities for pupils/students to be involved in the running of the library?

3.6b Information literacy and independent learning skills

The Chartered Institute of Library and Information Professionals defines information literacy as: *knowing when and why you need information, where to find it, and how to evaluate, use and communicate it in an ethical manner.*[7]

The school library may be excellent in its provision of learning resources. However, the ability to find, use and manipulate that information in the context of the teaching and learning in the classroom, is the key challenge for the library policy to address if it is to have an impact on the development of independent learning skills.

The skills to research and handle information need to be taught explicitly and practised regularly, in the context of real learning situations throughout the curriculum, not as discrete library lessons.

The library's role in this needs to be thought through:

- Is the library used to teach pupils about library classification schemes, subject indexes and catalogues?
- Are pupils encouraged to find and use resources independently?
- How do pupils develop confidence in using a range of information sources to retrieve information e.g. books, encyclopaedias and online?
- Does the library play a role in developing pupils' search skills with all formats of information, to maximise access and success rates?
- Have information handling skills been mapped across the curriculum to each year group so that they can be taught and reinforced in a planned way?
- Is access to appropriate resources provided for sixth form students undertaking research for EPQs? Are library staff involved in teaching the study skills element of the EPQ course?
- Is there evidence of library use in pupils' work? How is this collected and used for self-evaluation?
- Are all teachers involved in monitoring library use for their class of pupils/subject area?
- Are teachers able to set homework confident in the knowledge that pupils can access information sources at home, or in the school or public library?
- In primary schools, is there any library input to the information shared with partner secondary schools?
- What links have been established with neighbouring FE and HE institutions and their libraries?

---

[7] *https://infolit.org.uk/*

3.7 Monitoring and Evaluation

If the library is to reflect the life and priorities of the school on an ongoing basis, its role will need to be regularly reviewed and monitored. Mechanisms for monitoring and evaluating library provision should be included in the policy.

- How is the library's contribution going to be monitored, discussed and understood and supported by all the staff?
- If there is a computerised library management system, is the management information used to inform planning and future developments?
- Does the library feature in the school's development plan?
- Are funds clearly earmarked for library provision?
- Does the school identify library development priorities on an annual basis? Does the school have access to a Schools Library Service for advice regarding library provision? Does the school subscribe to School Library Association, a valuable source of guidance on running school libraries? If not, how does the school keep informed of best practice and national standards of library provision?

The whole-school community should be involved in the organisation of the library in order to further develop understanding of its role.

- Is there a governor with specific responsibility for library matters? Is the literacy governor kept informed of the library's role? Does the person responsible for library policy report to Governors' meetings on an annual basis?
- Are parents encouraged to visit the library? Are they involved in its running in any way?
- Are there opportunities for pupils to help? More than just tackling shelf-tidying chores, their involvement should be to foster both pride in, and responsibility for, library operations.

Step 4: Consult widely about your draft document

Pass your draft document (or relevant sections of it) to those who are affected by your policy, i.e. a cross-section of all your users. This means inviting comment which may highlight misunderstanding of what you do and how the library is used. Users' perspectives might not be yours. It is important to uncover and clarify existing practices and policies if your document is really to become a whole-school responsibility.

A practical approach to the consultation process could be:

1. Ask selected pupils for their opinions under the same headings that you have used and add their comments and perspectives to a second draft.
2. Give a copy of this draft to your line manager for comment.
3. With the head teacher's permission show your draft to the local Schools Library Service advisor for comment
4. Ask for the document to be discussed at a Senior Management Team Meeting.
5. Circulate the revised third draft to colleagues and invite comment within a fixed time period.

6. Amend as necessary and produce a final version. Include an outline of your consultation process and the people you consulted on the document, including the name of the head and your line manager. Add the date and the expected date of the next revision.

If you are lucky enough to be given INSET time to develop your policy, a possible approach would be:

1. Open the staff discussion with the key question: What defines our library and what is its purpose? Note the main responses to help you define aims – related to the wider aims of the school – and use this to write the opening section of your new policy.
2. Write, as questions, the major headings that you have already identified, onto flipchart paper and organise colleagues into groups to answer the questions. Circulate between groups to provide information and keep the task on track.
3. Use the flip-chart thinking to create a first draft.
4. Show the same headings to pupils – representatives from each year group – and gather their responses into a second draft.
5. Circulate the draft to all concerned and receive further comment within a clearly stated deadline.
6. Amend and produce final version.

Step 5: Publish your finished copy

The resulting policy should be widely shared in order that the philosophy, concepts, and intentions for practice and development are understood, endorsed, and ready to be put into practice.[8]

In the past we might have created a glossy printed copy of our library policy. But in this digital age that is no longer necessary or even advisable. Out-of-date copies in circulation do not give a good impression of your library or school.

As stated at the beginning of this guide, the policy is a working document that will be updated as people, practices and situations change. Most schools now log their policies in a high-profile folder on their intranet. Many policies will be available to the public, in particular parents. Your policy document should be loaded in the same folder.

The head teacher will decide whether it has public or staff-only access. Naturally as librarian you will recommend public access.

Step 6: Promote your policy document

Depending on its access status, you will send a link for the document to all staff, governors, parents and your Schools Library Service adviser.

---

[8] International Federation of Library Associations and Institutions (2015) *IFLA School Library Guidelines*, page 22. Viewed at https://www.ifla.org/files/assets/school-libraries-resource-centers/publications/ifla-school-library-guidelines.pdf [accessed 2/10/17]

If it is a large document, you may prefer to email a summary and explain how they can view the main document.

Step 7: Operate the Policy

A policy document by itself is not enough; it is the implementation of the policy that counts. All library practices should be carried out in line with the agreed policy. If there seems to be a persistent need to veer from policy in some aspect of provision, this indicates that part of the policy should be reviewed and another consultation process might be needed.

To keep the policy document at the forefront of thinking, take every opportunity to quote from it in displays, newsletters, curriculum booklets and, where necessary, letters to parents.

Step 8: Update/Revise

Revisit your policy every year as a matter of principle and amend as appropriate.

Carry out a more structured revision every two to three years in line with normal school procedures.

Archive the old policy as it is a useful historical document and you may wish to refer back to it in the future.

Examples of Library Policies are given in the Appendices at the end of this Guideline.

PART TWO: Library Development Plan

What is a Development Plan?

Whereas the policy considered principles and practices, the development plan (also called the improvement plan) is a schedule of clearly defined, agreed and costed tasks that the library will complete within a given timescale. It is usually planned in the shorter term for one year and also over a longer period, perhaps three years.

The purpose of the Library Development Plan

The plan shows how the school intends its library to become more effective in supporting teaching and learning, and how the library will support the attainment of whole-school targets.

It helps you to prioritise and set a timescale to achieve targets. It is a tool to demonstrate library progress to your senior management/leadership team and to justify spending. It helps you review library performance.

Links with the school development plan

Every school constantly changes and strives to improve. Each has its own School Improvement Plan with priorities for the coming months and years. The library, as a focus of learning in the school, should feature in it. Likewise, the Library Development should refer to the School Improvement Plan and reflect whole-school priorities.

How to write a Library Development Plan

There are 6 steps to consider:

1. Gather information and assess the current situation
2. Consult
3. Produce a draft
4. Seek agreement and submit final copy
5. Implement the plan
6. Revisit and Revise.

Step 1: Gather information and assess current situation

Study the School Development Plan for potential for library involvement in forthcoming school initiatives and curriculum changes. And do not forget to check whether the School Improvement Plan already has plans for the library. This must be followed through on the library plan.

Read the school's latest inspection report, noting the school's strengths and weaknesses and any course of action that the inspectors recommend.

Analyse any usage/non-usage statistics you have gathered, or attitude surveys undertaken, for indications of where library development efforts should be concentrated.

Refer back to the Policy document to review current working practices and provision. Consider the following questions:

- What works and what needs support and improvement?
- Is the library used effectively by staff and pupils – what changes would bring improvement?
- What training is needed by pupils, colleagues and by you to increase effectiveness?
- What new equipment is needed to develop library learning and teaching?
- What new/refurbished fixtures and fittings are needed to keep the library as the key centre for informational resource provision and as a welcoming place to read for pleasure?
- How could links with external agencies be improved and to what benefit to your library?

Hint: Timing

Also consider the timing of the next stage in the school development plan – so that it can include major elements of the plan you are about to create.

Hint: Further Reading

If you would like to see best practice examples that might be appropriate to select as targets on your own library plan, please refer to the following:

Successful Primary School Libraries: Case studies of good practice.[9] This contains six case study schools as examples of good practice and value-added provision, both urban and rural and of varying sizes and facing various challenges.

School Libraries: A literature review of current provision and evidence of impact.[10] This literature review provides a comprehensive picture of current library provision in the UK. It gives a review of the known impact of school libraries on pupils' skills, motivation and enjoyment, and outlines the elements that make a good school library.

Making a Start with your Primary School Library.[11] This is an SLA back-to-basics guide that is a must-read for anyone new to running a primary school library or whose library is currently underdeveloped.

New Beginnings: A Practical Guide to Taking Charge of a Secondary School Library.[12] This provides similar advice for those new to running a secondary library.

A whole range of other useful guides are available from the School Library Association website.[13]

---

[9] Greenwood, Helen, Creaser, Claire and Maynard, Sally (2008) *Successful Primary School Libraries: Case studies of good practice.* Booktrust. Viewed at http://www.lboro.ac.uk/microsites/infosci/lisu/downloads/successful-prim-sch-libs.pdf [accessed 3/10/17]

[10] Teravainen, Anne and Clark, Christina (2017) *School Libraries: A literature review of current provision and evidence of impact.* National Literacy Trust. https://literacytrust.org.uk/research-services/research-reports/school-libraries-literature-review-current-provision-and-evidence-impact-2017/ [accessed 3/10/17]

[11] Duncan, Sally (2010) *Making a Start with your Primary School Library.* School Library Association

[12] Taylor, Laura (2017) *New Beginnings: A Practical Guide to Taking Charge of a Secondary School Library.* School Library Association

[13] http://www.sla.org.uk/publications-list.php [accessed 5/4/18]

Self-evaluation tools

In the long-term, a more structured approach to self-evaluation is recommended. Although now archived, the following are two excellent tools:

Improve your Library: a Self-Evaluation Process for Primary Schools.[14]

Improve your library: a self-evaluation process for secondary school libraries and learning resource centres.[15]

A more recent publication to consider is *How Good is Our School Library?*[16] Developed by the Scottish Library and Information Council with the support of a working group of school library experts, it aims to support every school to deliver a visionary school library. Aimed more at the secondary school sector but relevant to primary schools too.

Step 2: Consult

Allocate time to consult pupils and staff to gain their views of how the library should be developed. Ask them the same questions listed under Step 1 and gather opinions and ideas.

Ask your non-users how the library could become more attractive and useful to them.

Discuss your ideas and those you have gathered with your line manager and draw up a realistic set of priorities.

Discuss your proposed plan with your head teacher who will provide the strategic support and finance to lead the developments.

Step 3: Produce a draft

Many development plans are in landscape format, set out in tabular form.

As with the policy document, it is best to adopt the agreed school style and use school-defined headings. A library development plan that explicitly supports whole-school aims and is presented in the same language as the school improvement plan is more likely to be understood. And any accompanying funding bids are more likely to be listened to and accepted.

Likely headings include:

- Targets
- Success Criteria (i.e. the evidence that you have met your target)
- Realistic financial costs
- Training Needs (to achieve the targets)
- Key personnel (i.e. who is responsible for the various tasks)

---

[14] Department for Education and Skills (2004) *Improve your Library: a Self-Evaluation Process for Primary Schools.* DfES. Viewed at http://dera.ioe.ac.uk/5293/1/Self-evaluation%20process%20for%20Primary%20school%20libraries.pdf [accessed 3/10/17]

[15] Department for Education and Skills (2004) *Improve your library: a self-evaluation process for secondary school libraries and learning resource centres.* DfES. Viewed at https://101tips.files.wordpress.com/2008/01/self-evaluation-process-for-secondary-school-libraries-and-lrcs.pdf [accessed 10/11/17]

[16] Scottish Library and Information Council (2017) *How Good is Our School Library?* SLIC. Viewed at http://scottishlibraries.org/media/1665/hgiosls-pdf.pdf [accessed 4/10/17]

Length may vary, often three or four pages of A4 paper, but bear in mind the plan is not an endless wish list, rather a set of realistic targets.

Step 4: Seek agreement and submit final copy

Discuss your draft with the Senior Management Team. Explain how it links to whole-school planned developments. If necessary, highlight what might happen if the developments do not take place.

As with the Library Policy, load the Library Development Plan in the appropriate folder on the school's intranet and then notify staff, governors, the local Schools Library Service etc.

Step 5: Implement the plan

Break the plan down into termly targets and display these prominently in the library. (Publicising targets is a great incentive towards making them happen.) Tick them off as they are achieved. If any targets are not met, transfer them to the next term's plan. This keeps targets firmly in focus.

Step 6: Review and Revise

Review your Development Plan annually – in line with school procedures.

As you created the format when you wrote your first plan, updating it subsequently should be straightforward. Outstanding targets can be retained on the next plan and new ones added.

Archive the old plan for future reference.

Examples of Library Development Plans are given with policy documents in the Appendices to this guide.

Appendix 1

Dean Close Preparatory School

Library Policies and Development Plan

Policy written by **Rachel Sargeant** B.LIB Hons, MA, DMS, MCLIP, Preparatory School Librarian.

Created 18/4/2016, updated 13/3/17.

Dean Close Preparatory School (DCPS) is an independent school in Cheltenham, Gloucestershire with approximately 300 pupils, including 60 boarders.

The school library supports the strategic intent of Dean Close Prep School:

- Pastoral – a caring place where there is trust and where relationships are developed
- Academic – encourage creativity, independence of thought and initiative, and to provide pupils with a body of knowledge of lasting value
- Co-curricular – to have a range of activity suitable to develop talents in our young people.

1. Library Aims

1. To encourage the enjoyment of reading in a wide range of genres
2. To support teaching and learning in school
3. To develop pupils' independent learning skills

1.1 To encourage the enjoyment of reading in a wide range of genres:

- providing resources to encourage reading for pleasure and to support pupils' leisure interests (See Library Stock Management Policy)
- running a programme of library/reading promotion lessons and events for all year groups
- in consultation with English and Learning Support departments, providing appropriately challenging fiction to enable pupils to develop their reading and writing skills
- creating displays to highlight new stock and promote particular themes, often tied in with national initiatives
- ensuring the library stock is attractive by withdrawing tatty, out of date titles and creating some face-on, as opposed to all spine-on, shelf arrangements
- supporting departmental initiatives, for example author visits.

1.2 To support teaching and learning in school by:

- providing and maintaining resources to support the curriculum (See Library Stock Management Policy)

- consulting with Heads of Department and other teachers to develop and edit subject areas
- Providing short-term project boxes for classroom learning
- responding to new curriculum initiatives and encouraging Heads of Departments to involve the library at the planning stage
- informing teachers of new resources relevant to their subject
- offering a library induction session to new staff.

1.3 To develop pupils' independent learning skills by:

- providing assistance to pupils in the library
- delivering induction sessions in the library to all year groups as part of their English course
- equipping pupils with the skills to become information literate. Information literacy is "Knowing when and why you need information, where to find it, and how to evaluate, use and communicate in an ethical manner" (Source: CILIP 2004 in Culford). The library works with subject departments to deliver study skills training specific to their topics
- ensuring all sections of the library are clearly guided using, as far as possible, the same subject terms that are used in the school curriculum
- displaying all non-fiction stock (i.e. lending and reference) for each curriculum area together in guided and classified sections.

2. Accommodation

Situated between the Ferguson and Rickerby buildings on the ground floor, the library has space for a maximum of 50 pupils. There are two computer terminals, two study tables that each seat six pupils and one that seats two. There are two window seats and also beanbags for recreational reading. (DfES Building Bulletin 98 recommends that the school library should be able to seat 10% of its pupils. We can seat approximately 20 children; another 30 children sit on the floor.)

At break the library sometimes becomes full and the librarian has to ask pupils to leave.

3. Opening Hours

The library opens at break and lunch time Monday to Friday when the librarian or a colleague are on duty. Pupils can visit during the school day, Monday to Saturday, if accompanied or sent by a member of staff.

4. Use of the Library

The library is used by:

- pupils to choose books during supervised class visits and at break and lunchtimes
- Library skills lessons and Reader Development events led by the librarian
- Class groups booked in by teachers
- Year 8 Learning Support private study
- EAL booked lessons.

The library is **not** a common room for noisy chat, card games, computer games.

5. Role of the Librarian

The librarian is professionally qualified and experienced in librarianship and is a chartered member of CILIP (Chartered Institute of Library and Information Professionals). The current postholder is a masters graduate with a postgraduate Diploma in Management Studies.

The librarian is employed for 25 hours per week during term time plus three weeks per year.

The role of the librarian is to:

- organise and manage the library and its resources to meet the needs of the school's curriculum and to support the reading, learning and information requirements of the pupils
- help pupils with their reading and study queries
- supervise the use of computers in the library
- initiate and deliver annual induction programmes for each year group
- develop the information retrieval skills of pupils, enabling them to access information effectively in both electronic and paper form
- initiate and participate in activities to promote wider reading
- be responsible for the selection, maintenance and withdrawal of library stock across all subject areas and, where necessary, in consultation with Heads of Department
- be responsible for and monitor the library budget
- catalogue and classify the book stock
- operate the circulation system for all items borrowed and returned by school users, including dealing with overdue items and reservations.

The librarian reports to Head of Junior Forms. To maintain professional awareness, the librarian attends meetings and courses run by the Gloucestershire Library Service for Education and reads widely in the professional press.

6. Reading Ambassadors

Application procedure:

- Pupils in Year 8 write a letter of application to the librarian in September
- Interview with librarian.

Job Purpose: To promote reading and the library throughout the School.

Job Description (all tasks under the direction of the librarian):

1. Pass information from the Library to Houses
    - Promote authors/series
    - Give news about events, e.g. World Book Day
2. Pass information from Houses to the Library
    - Book recommendations
    - Suggestions for improving the Library

3. Read books at librarian's request and give an assessment of their interest/age range
4. Write short reviews and articles for Hermes and other outlets
5. Help with stock selection (choosing from publishers' catalogues)
6. Help with deselection (removing unpopular titles from the shelves)
7. Plan new Reading and Library initiatives
8. Attend weekly duties in the library during break or lunch.

7. Rules

- pupils must not bring food or drink into the library
- as the library is designated as an area for quiet reading and study, noisy pupils will be asked to go into the playground
- at all times library users must show consideration to others who are working quietly
- the library computers are for school work or checking emails only, no games
- pupils refusing to follow library rules will be reported to their House Master or Mistress

8. Evaluation

The librarian monitors library use by:

- keeping records of pupils visiting the library
- generating statistical reports from the library computerised circulation.

The librarian takes account of this evidence to assess the library's impact on pupils' learning. She will evaluate its activities by:

- reporting in writing to the Deputy Head (Academic) on annual library performance
- engaging pupils and staff in discussions about the library
- comparing statistics with previous years
- consulting staff and pupils on a department by department basis to monitor current attitudes towards, and use of, the library
- reviewing the annual library development plan to see how tasks have been achieved
- reviewing key areas on a rolling programme with reference to *Improve Your Library: A Self-Evaluation Process For the Primary School Library*.

9. Bibliography

Barret, Lynn and Douglas, Jonathan (2004) CILIP guidelines for secondary schools

Dewe, Michael (2007) Ideas and Designs: Creating the Environment for the Primary School Library SLA Guidelines

DfES (2004) Building Bulletin 98: Building Framework for Secondary School Projects

DfES (2004) Improve Your Library: Self-Evaluation for the Primary School Library

DfES (2004) Improve Your Library: A Self-Evaluation Process for Secondary School Libraries and Learning Resource Centres

Good School Libraries (2006) www.ofsted.gov.uk

SLA **Guidelines:** Priority Paperwork

In preparing this document, policies from the following schools were consulted via the School Library Association website:

Culford Senior School, Suffolk (Lesley Martin)

The King's School (L.Dawes)

Lea Valley High School and Sports College, Enfield (Helen Roberts)

Licensed Victuallers' School, Berkshire (Sue Bastone)

Pembroke School (Liz Smith).

Dean Close Preparatory School

Library Stock Management Policy

1. Purpose of the Library Stock

To offer a current, relevant and accessible selection of resources

- to pupils for leisure reading and in support of their studies
- to teachers in support of their teaching

2. Stock Coverage

The library provides the following resources:

2.1 Fiction

- Teenage fiction for Yr7 – 8 (denoted by a red dot on the spine)
- Children's fiction available to all years, especially Yr 5 – 6
- Younger fiction for Yr 3 – 4
- Classics (children's and some adult)
- Graphic novels
- Christian fiction (and non-fiction)

2.2 Non-fiction

- Non-fiction to support the KS2 and KS3 curriculum
- General non-fiction for leisure reading
- Browser books – Guinness Book of Records, Star Wars annuals etc. – for leisure reading

2.3 Reference stock

- dictionaries, atlases, encyclopaedias and other non-fiction titles to support studies and general interest

Subject-specific reference books are interfiled in the main Categorized Dewey sequence.

2.4 Periodicals

- First News – weekly children's newspaper
- How It Works – monthly science magazine

- Aquila
- The Week Junior

2.5 CDs

- Audio versions of children's fiction to listen to in the library on a Coomber CD player.

Junior forms and Yr 6 – 8 English classrooms have collections of fiction and non-fiction for pupils to read in the classroom, purchased by Head of Junior Forms/English teachers. Each boarding house offers a fiction library, purchased by house masters/mistresses.

3. Selection Criteria

The librarian, as the library budget holder, decides whether to purchase a book, using the following criteria:

Authority

- Reputation of author/publisher
- Accuracy of content

Scope and treatment

- In-depth treatment or overview
- Intended age range
- Quality of illustration and layout
- Ease of use, contents page, index, glossary

Format

- Suitable for repeat borrowing
- Sturdy pages and binding

Collection balance

- Does the book fill a stock gap?
- Does the book present an alternative view of a subject?
- Does it enhance the cultural diversity of the collection?
- Does it contain positive images of people with disabilities?

Value for Money

- Does the value of the item to the pupils and staff justify its cost?

Multiple copies

- The librarian will purchase more than one copy of a book if demand for it is high and likely to remain so over time. Subject departments purchase multiple copies of textbooks and set texts.

4. Donations

Donations of second-hand books are generally not encouraged as they are: rarely in good enough condition for library use; out of date; or duplicate current stock.

5. Censorship

All library stock is published by mainstream publishers and is deemed worthy for publication in the United Kingdom. Some titles, in the Year 7–8 Fiction section, are challenging reads, beyond most pupils' experience and designed to broaden their understanding. Pupils are free to borrow any book, except that Year 7–8 Fiction is limited to these age groups. Occasionally – when a Year 6 pupil wishes to borrow a Year7 title – the librarian will ask a pupil to obtain written parental permission before releasing it.

6. Selection Sources

The librarian identifies potential new titles in the following ways:

- book reviews in *The School Librarian*, newspapers and magazines
- recommendations from staff and pupils
- Fiction Forum meetings with other Gloucestershire school librarians
- book award winners and shortlists (where appropriate and appealing)
- identified stock gaps
- visits to bookshops and other libraries
- publishers' catalogues and websites.

7. Stock Maintenance

The librarian weeds and maintains the stock to ensure it remains current, relevant and attractive.

Criteria for withdrawal:

- in poor condition
- information no longer current
- topic no longer on the curriculum
- not borrowed or consulted in the last three years.

The librarian consults the appropriate subject departments where it is unclear if the above criteria apply to a particular title.

Withdrawn stock is disposed of on site. Stock no longer suitable for the library is unlikely to be suitable elsewhere. When stock is withdrawn in bulk, it will be offered to Better World Books, providing an early collection date can be agreed.

Stock maintenance includes identifying stock gaps. If new stock cannot be bought immediately, gaps are flagged up as a development need on the Library Development Plan.

8. Stock Control

The library uses Eclipse for its computerised circulation system.

8.1 Loan Allowances

Pupils may borrow two books for three weeks, renewable twice.

Staff may borrow books and renew them as necessary by negotiation.

8.2 Overdue books

Procedures for dealing with overdue books are explained on the Overdue Library Books Policy.

The library does not charge fines.

Overdue notices to staff are sent out every term.

9. Current Stock Levels

Total stock: 4790

General children's fiction: 1080

Year 7–8 fiction: 630

Young fiction: 440

Classic: 90

Non-fiction: 2400 (including 440 reference titles)

Christian books: 150

As all the books were added to the system in 2012, it is not possible to calculate the age of the stock.

10. Budget

The annual library budget is approximately £XXXX to spend on books, online resources, CDs and periodicals. This equates to just under £XX per pupil*. There are separate school budgets for stationery and equipment.

Booktrust worked with LISU at Loughborough University to recommend expenditure per head on library books of £10 for primary schools. This figure is for fiction and non-fiction and does not include set texts, textbooks or study guides. The figure is due to be updated. The recommended figure for secondary schools is £15 per head.

Dean Close Preparatory School Library Development Plan 2016/17 prepared by Rachel Sargeant

DEVELOPMENT	SUCCESS CRITERIA	STAFF	COSTS
To encourage reading for pleasure			
• Hold induction sessions for every class by end of Sept 16	Improved library usage by all year groups	RS	
• Set up and give a monthly pitch for Circulating Collections for Years 3 to 5	Completed review cards. Feedback from form tutors. Pupils visiting library for sequels	RS, Yr3/4/5 teachers	
• Implement Yr 6 Reading Passport Programme	Yr6 pupils read in a variety of genres	RS, JLT	
• Develop rolling programme of promotional tasks for Yr8 Reading Ambassadors	Programme up and running, positive feedback from house parents, more pupils using the library	RS, Reading Ambassadors, house parents	Posters and stationery £100
• Develop rolling programme of promotional boards in library, around school, in classrooms	More pupils reading recommended titles	RS, Reading Ambassadors	
• Hold fortnightly reading for pleasure sessions with Year 3	Year 3 pupils read in a variety of genres and visit the library to read	RS, Yr3 teachers and teaching assistants	
• To hold events in support of What the Dickens Weeks and WBD	Yr 3 able to create and write a memorable character. Yr5 familiar with A Christmas Carol	RS, Yr 3 and 5 teachers	
• Investigate using the Eclipse system to promote titles	Yr 5 to 8 using online catalogue and posting reviews	RS, Reading Ambassadors	
To develop pupils' study skills			
• Hold fortnightly library skills sessions for Yr 3	Yr 3 secure in how to use school library, alphabetical order, indexes, contents, glossaries, able to carry out basic research	RS, Yr 3 teachers and teaching assistants	
• Observe colleagues' lessons in English, drama, geography, science with a view to seeing how library skills sessions could complement subject lessons	Programme agreed for next year	RS, Yr 6-8 teachers	

SLA Guidelines: Priority Paperwork

To improve library provision			
• Order and take delivery of new fiction shelving to create face-on display	Improved use of fiction stock	RS	£2252
• Devise and implement a system to chase up overdue books so that popular titles are not out of circulation for long periods of time	System implemented, fewer overdues	RS, SMT, house parents	
Other Developments			
• To investigate the 'clickview' online library system with a view to managing this for DCPS in the future.	Plan agreed for next year	RS, ZS	
• To take advantage of CPD opportunities	Relevant courses attended and training implemented in the workplace	RS, GLOSLIBS	
• To manage Eclipse library circulation system and modify it to meet DCPS needs	System running smoothly. Online interactive catalogue used by pupils.	RS, GLOSLIBS	Cost to be met by this year DCS

Appendix 2

Notre Dame School Library Case Study and Policy
Creating and Implementing a Primary School Library Policy

Anne Thompson BSc (Econ) CertTESOL (Trinity) Prep School Librarian (2000 – 2017).

Notre Dame School is an Independent school in Surrey for girls aged 2-18 and boys aged 2-7.

I was appointed Prep School Librarian at Notre Dame School in February 2000. This was a new position at the school, required in connection with the setting up of a library in its new location in September of that year. The school was also due to be inspected within the coming year. This was quite a daunting task. Although it may be imagined that spending time on the preparation of paperwork would not be a priority in these circumstances, in reality I found that the task of creating a Library Policy served to make the job both less daunting and, in the long term, more successful.

Initially I spent a little while trying to ascertain exactly what the senior management team hoped their library would offer to both pupils and staff. Prior to drawing up a draft policy I had discussions with the Deputy Head (my line manager) and the Head of English about the role of the library within the school. However the policy had to be an accurate reflection of the current position and not a vision of an ideal library that we hoped to create in the future. This was to be viewed as a working document providing a foundation on which I could build to improve the library and its role within the school. The policy would, I hoped, highlight areas that needed to be included in a development plan.

Before I started work on the policy itself I also assessed the library's current collection of resources and started work on cataloguing new stock that teachers had already bought. This helped me to have a more accurate picture of what was available currently. Informal discussions with class teachers also helped to ascertain what needed to be in place in readiness for the opening of the library in six months time. This also assisted with the content of the policy itself.

In addition I found it useful to examine the job description provided by the school for the Librarian role as any specific requirements of the post, such as teaching of information literacy/supporting reading/classroom assistance/additional duties, needed to be incorporated in the library's policy too. It was at this point that I attended a one-day course on "Preparing the School Library for Inspection" and this proved invaluable as the importance of documentation was included and we were provided with examples. As a new member of the School Library Association I also consulted the guidelines available at that time, *Establishing a Primary School Library Policy*, J Dunne, 1994, which I found extremely helpful.

I had seen examples of library policies created for other schools and although I found these useful as a guide to structure and suggested content I did try not to follow them too slavishly as each school is different. The most successful school libraries are those that accurately meet the needs of their own particular users so I believed it was vital that this new library would be effective for this particular school and the pupils and staff who worked there. The school's mission statement was to be included in the policy and it is very important that the library policy, and indeed the library, reflect the school's ethos. The pastoral element of the library and the way in which it contributes to the education and moral welfare of the pupils is, I believe, extremely important and I wanted to ensure that this was incorporated into the policy too.

By now I had an idea of the current situation regarding the library and its short term future but before I started to incorporate this into a draft policy I read some of the existing policies for other subjects and departments. This was partly so that I could get a feel of the "house style" so that the Library Policy read as an integral part of the whole school documentation but also so that I could check that any links to other policies were highlighted. I felt, initially at least, that this was particularly important in connection with the English Policy.

Once I had created a draft policy I submitted this to the Head teacher and the senior management team for their feedback. The details of the new library accommodation including the IT already bought and installed was included in this draft. After amendments were made, and a further consultation with my line manager and the Head of English completed, the first Library Policy was finalised and made available for all staff in the following Autumn Term to coincide with the opening of the new library. It was also, fortunately, ready for the visiting inspectors the following March.

This was just the beginning of the Library Policy's life. Within another twelve months a new head teacher was appointed and a new whole-school five year improvement plan was put in place. Any library policy should ideally be reviewed every year or so but these events provided an excellent opportunity to ensure that both the Library Policy and Library Development Plan reflected and actively contributed to the new school improvement plan. I was now able to use the new SLA publication *Policy Making and Development Planning for the Primary School Library*, K. Harrison, (2001) which contained more detail and an extremely helpful Framework for Creating a Library Policy. (This publication was subsequently updated in 2007 by K. Harrison and T. Adams.)

Although having to update paperwork can at times feel like a chore, it does serve to focus the librarian's attention on what needs to be done. Updating the policy as a result of targets on the development plan being reached or changes being made to accommodation, resources or the librarian's role reinforces the view that the library is not stagnating but continues to reflect the needs of the community. Anything that raises the profile of the library and the role it plays in the school's achievements has to be a good thing.

At each annual review I collaborated with other members of staff to ensure that links with other policies were highlighted and still relevant. It is possible to use the updating of the policy to make sure that all staff are aware of changes to the library and what it offers them. Ideally they should already know about these but it never hurts to reinforce them and sometimes seeing it written down draws attention to all that is available in the school library. Regular consultation with both staff and pupils is vital so that you have a user's perspective on the library and regular updating of the policy facilitates this. In addition to attending meetings and informal discussions I have also on occasion used questionnaires completed by both pupils and teachers. This has proved an invaluable source of feedback and has resulted in changes being made such as an emphasis on increasing resources for a particular area of non-fiction and the setting up of a book club.

The Library Policy can also act as a promotion tool and should be made available to all staff. Once I had updated the policy each year and any changes were agreed by the senior management team, the policy was put on Firefly (the school Virtual Learning Environment) so that all staff had access to it. It can be a useful reference point when clarification is needed regarding use of resources, charging for lost books, booking of library space and so forth.

As librarian at the school for seventeen years additional changes, such as a further move to new premises, providing resources and library visits for our expanding school nursery, increased involvement with the Humanities teaching (referred to by the acronym TASK at Notre Dame) and the adoption of Accelerated Reader, have necessitated further changes to the policy. These mean that the policy is quite a bit longer than it was initially, however I have tried to keep it as succinct as possible. It should be easy to read and refer to in order to be effective and useful to other staff. I originally used the headings suggested by J Dunne in his 1994 publication and have largely kept to these ever since. However I have seen other examples that work well and some incorporate an Information Literacy or Collection Policy too. At Notre Dame School there is a separate Reading Policy so elements that may normally appear in a Library Policy are not required. The same applies to information literacy as this is included in the Humanities (TASK) Policy. I mention this simply to illustrate that library policies can vary greatly, largely to fit in with their school's requirements. The most important thing is that it works for you and your school.

As preparation for writing this case study I looked back at the first policy that I created and compared it to the most recent and it was a revelation. Because change and growth has been gradual, I had not appreciated quite how much of it there has been. I have found the policy useful on occasions to identify my own personal targets as part of the staff appraisal programme too.

In July 2017 I retired from my position as Prep School Librarian and was able to hand the Library Policy on to my successor; in the hope that it would act as a valuable tool, it sets out clearly how this particular library is used and operates. The policy should answer many of her questions about her new role. It provides her with a starting point on which to improve and develop the library further in the future.

Bibliography

DUNNE, JOHN, (1994) *Establishing a Primary School Library Policy.* School Library Association

HARRISON, KAY (2001) *Policy Making and Development Planning for the Primary School Library.* School Library Association

HARRISON, KAY and ADAMS, TRICIA (2007) *Policy Making and Development Planning for the Primary School Library.* School Library Association

NATIONAL LITERACY TRUST *School Libraries: A Plan for Improvement* (2010) https://literacytrust.org.uk/policy-and-campaigns/all-party-parliamentary-group-literacy/school-library-commission/ (accessed 23/10/2017)

SLA Guidelines: Priority Paperwork

Notre Dame School Library
Library Policy

'An effective school library acting as a power house of learning and reading within a school is a unique resource.'

—*School Libraries: A Plan for Improvement* – National Literacy Trust, 2010

The Role of the Library

Pupils need to develop appropriate learning strategies thereby becoming independent, lifelong learners. To assist them in this aim we must remember that 'we are all educators accompanying young people in their efforts to build their lives for today and tomorrow', in accordance with the school's stated Mission.

The school library's role is to help create confident, enthusiastic readers and to engage children in life-long learning. At Notre Dame School we aim to provide a lively, welcoming and well-resourced school library, which will give all pupils a broad and positive experience of books, computers and other media.

The library should support the Reading Policy at Notre Dame by endeavouring to provide sufficient high quality literature to give enough challenging material to suit all ability levels. The pupils should be made aware of the wide range of literature available and encouraged to see reading as an enjoyable and rewarding pastime. In addition the library and its stock contribute to the spiritual, moral, social and cultural development of the pupils by providing resources covering a range of issues pertaining to both the PSHE curriculum and our values.

Library Provision

Accommodation and Access

- There is one library situated in the main school building, Burwood House, for use by the whole Prep section of the school from Nursery to Year 6. The central fiction and non-fiction collections are housed here.
- Each class teacher is given an allocation of up to 50 books to be withdrawn from the library, which may then be retained in the classroom. These can be fiction to supplement their class library or non-fiction to support teaching and learning. This, together with the individual borrowing by each child, should ensure that all books remain in circulation and all pupils have access to the library resources.
- The Library is open daily from 8.40 until 4.00
- From Nursery to Year 6 the pupils have weekly library lessons when they may change their library books. Junior pupils may also visit the library to exchange library books at other times at the discretion of their class teacher and the librarian.
- Reading support and guided reading sessions run by the librarian for girls in the Junior Department are also timetabled to take place in the library.
- The timetable showing opening times and available lesson times is available on

Outlook and updated regularly. In addition the library and the librarian may be booked for TASK sessions, research for a particular subject or reading promotion lessons. These bookings should be made on Outlook with an accompanying email sent to the librarian outlining the requirements in the way of resources etc.

- Girls in Year 6 may visit the senior library during one afternoon break each week allowing them access to a greater range of material.
- During afternoon activity breaks the Prep Library is used for quiet reading, selecting books, individual research and completing Accelerated Reader quizzes. If the library is very busy, priority will be given to the year group whose turn it is that day.
- In addition to the four networked computers in the library the school i-Pads, stored in the ICT suite may be booked for use in the library.

Staffing
- The full time school librarian supervises the Library.
- Library prefects are selected from Year 6 to assist the librarian in the library with shelving, book covering, issuing books and other routine tasks.

Funding
- The library receives funding in the form of an annual budget allocation, which is reviewed on a yearly basis. Provided finances permit, this should allow for expansion, in order that the school is able to meet the guidelines set, and also the renewal of 10% of worn or outdated stock each year. Commission earned at the Book Fairs held regularly at the school supplements this allocation.

Organisation and Use

- The library is divided into two sections; a teaching area comprising SMART Board, networked computers and two large tables for group work and a reading area with seating and additional cushions.
- The non-fiction resources are classified according to the Dewey system and are clearly labelled on the spine. Fiction is arranged alphabetically by the author's surname.
- The school uses a web based library management system, Junior Librarian.Net that includes cataloguing and loan functions.
- Each pupil is allowed to borrow two books from the library at any one time and encouraged to use both the fiction and non-fiction sections. Girls in Years 5 and 6 may borrow 3 books to allow them a wider range of reading material. Year 6 girls may borrow an additional book from the senior library.
- Books may be borrowed for a period of three weeks and overdue notices are forwarded on a regular basis to class teachers by the librarian via e-mail.
- Parents are notified of outstanding books from the previous term and are charged for books not returned or replaced by a given date.
- The library prefects are trained to use the on-line system and the girls are encouraged to use Junior Librarian.net to retrieve information about the books available.
- At Notre Dame the library is seen as the focus of reading development and book promotion. Activities are arranged such as author/illustrator visits, contact with our own

- Patron of Reading, special activities linked to national initiatives such as World Book Day, National Poetry Day and Children's Book Week. Regular book fairs are organised to promote current children's fiction.
- There is a weekly Chatterbooks Book Club run by the librarian for girls in Years 5 and 6 where reading is promoted through activities, discussion, quizzes, author interviews and games.
- The librarian teaches children how to use the library. The pupils are given a basic introduction to the layout of the library and how to find the various resources. Over a period of time the girls will learn how to make full use of the library and to handle information, both from books and ICT, effectively. The aim is to ensure that by the time pupils leave Notre Dame they are equipped with the necessary skills to become lifelong, independent learners. This supports the teaching of Information Literacy as outlined in the TASK Policy.
- Class teachers are provided with details of resources available for each new TASK topic both in the library itself and on-line by the librarian.
- A staff guide to the library is available in both print and on-line format. This guide outlines how the library is organised and gives brief information about the resources available.
- Information and news from the Prep Library is provided by the librarian for inclusion in the school's weekly Friday mailing newsletter.
- The Prep Library has a Twitter account with regular updates from the library and the world of children's books.

Resources

- The school aims to provide resources that provide a balance between supporting the curriculum and meeting individual needs and interests. It is hoped that the range of stock held in the library will both inspire and challenge all pupils.
- The librarian has overall responsibility for selection. However all teachers, especially subject heads, are consulted on a regular basis in order to ensure that their needs are being met.
- There is a stock of audio-books in CD format that may be borrowed by pupils and staff. In addition the library has a supply of DVDs for use by teachers. The Library also subscribes to several magazines and junior newspaper editions. Back issues of *The Week Junior* are catalogued and available for loan to teachers for use in the classroom. Supplies of *First News* may be also be borrowed.
- The condition of all stock is continually monitored and stock is withdrawn when it becomes worn or outdated.
- The librarian provides the Head of ICT with details of apps for use on the school i-Pads both for literacy and creative use in the classroom.
- The on-line resources available on the four networked computers in the Junior Library include:

    a). Junior Librarian Net – the online library management system

    b). Firefly – Notre Dame VLE – the Prep Library has its own area on the VLE with areas devoted to new books, library news and information. The Research Area of the VLE provides links for each Junior year group including World Book for Kids, an on-line Encyclopaedia to which the library subscribes and additional pre-selected websites. There is a specific teacher resource area that includes the library guide and further links.

c). Accelerated Reader – on-line reading management programme that enables the librarian and English teachers to effectively monitor the reading progress of pupils in the Junior Department. Pupils complete regular Star Reader tests to assess their reading ability and their reading age. Pupils are guided to books at an appropriate reading level and then complete comprehension quizzes in either the library or classroom via the internet. The librarian provides the Director of Studies and individual class teachers with Accelerated Reader report material which aids the assessment and monitoring of pupil progress.

Early Years Foundation Stage

- Pupils from the Nursery visit the library each week accompanied by their teachers.
- The younger children are able to listen to stories and rhymes building on their listening skills and familiarising them with the library environment.
- The older Nursery children are guided as to how to choose appropriate books and are able to select a book to take home to share with their parents each visit.
- All the children are taught how to care for books and encouraged to view reading as an enjoyable and rewarding pastime.

Monitoring and Evaluation

- The on-line library management system is used to monitor borrowing figures and provide information regarding the use of stock.
- Members of staff are asked for feedback regarding gaps in stock and suggestions for development of new curriculum areas.
- Following staff discussion the information gathered from the monitoring of the libraries is used in the production of a library development plan.

Updated: Sep 2016   Review: Sep 2017

Appendix 3

Clayesmore Prep School
Library Policies

Heather Bignold, Librarian

Clayesmore School is an independent school for boys and girls of the English public school tradition in the village of Iwerne Minster, Dorset, England.

Library Policy

Objectives

Our aim is that the school library should be a whole-school resource providing essential support for the curriculum, as well as enhancing the academic and social development of the individual.

It should actively support teaching and learning, promote the development of information skills and encourage intellectual curiosity.

The library is seen as a complementary resource for the school, working alongside Computing.

We hope that through use of the library, children will develop an enjoyment of reading for pleasure and relaxation. (There is a separate statement for this.)

We want all pupils to leave the school able to use the library independently for study and leisure.

Location

The library is situated on the first floor of the Prep-School building making it central to the school. The room is informally divided into two areas: a fiction library which also houses the audio collection and magazines / comics, which is furnished with beanbags and cushions for relaxed reading. There are also facilities for display. The non-fiction area of the library is arranged around two large tables where studying can be carried out. Most reference material is shelved within the range of non-fiction.

Stock

- There are approximately 4,700 book items in the library (May 2017). This includes fiction, non-fiction and Reference.
- All non-fiction (including the reference) is classified according to a junior version of Dewey. Subject indexes are provided to help the pupils access the books. Extra copies of this index have been bought for classrooms, so that pupils can refer to them while working and preparing to use the library.
- At present the audio collection is not on the catalogue. The library has approximately 200 audio items in the collection.

- The book collection is weighted towards fiction, but the non-fiction collection is constantly being added to using recommendations from staff and requests from pupils. There is a growing collection of 'faction' books (*Horrible Histories*, etc.) which are very popular with the children. These are classified, but are kept together rather than scattered through the collection.
- Many Heads of Department keep their own subject libraries within their classroom. These are not catalogued centrally.

Other Resources

New magazines and comics are purchased regularly, and a daily paper *(The Times)* is also kept in the library. We have a subscription to *First News* which includes access to extra online resources and to *The Week Junior*. Some periodicals are donated by members of staff.

Staffing

The school employs a chartered librarian on a part-time basis (currently 29 hours per week in term-time). There is close liaison with the Head of English, and all heads of department and other staff are consulted when ordering new stock.

Pupil librarians chosen from Year 8 help on a regular basis. Their duties include helping to process new stock, notifying other pupils about reserved and overdue items, and overseeing the desk during lunchtimes.

Membership is held to the School Library Association

Use and Access

The library is open all day. All forms have the opportunity to have timetabled lessons in the library, and pupils are also free to visit the library at any other time (with regard to use by other classes), including the evenings and weekends. It is not possible to staff the library for all of this time.

Pupils may borrow two books and one audio item at any one time. Books can be kept for three weeks and audio items for one. Reference stock cannot usually be borrowed. (Staff can borrow a greater number of books and keep them for longer).

Promotion

The librarian, with other staff, promotes the uses of the library for information and pleasure. Displays are done to celebrate literacy events (e.g. World Book Day, Children's Book Week) and also to encourage the discovery of different genres, e.g. adventure stories, poetry. Authors and illustrators are also invited into the school on a regular basis (approx. two visits per year), which is a great encouragement to the children with their reading. Some liaising over such visits takes place with local schools.

There is an automated library system in place – Junior Librarian. As well as handling the routine issuing and discharging of books, it allows staff to monitor use of the library as a whole and also by individuals.

There is now a second computer in the library with this system on so that pupils can see what is available, write reviews and request books.

Funding

The budget for each academic year is allocated by the Head of Prep. There is also a separate budget for author visits.

Monitoring and Evaluation

Use of the library is monitored informally by the librarian and other staff. More formal information on library use can be obtained from Junior Librarian for books, and by manual recording for the CDs.

Informal discussion with staff is a very useful means of monitoring and evaluating library use.

Heather Bignold, May 2017.

Library Selection Policy

It is intended that the materials in the library should provide a balanced selection for all the children in the school; this will include materials suitable for the less able children as well as those who are more able.

All children use the library from Nursery through to Year 8. Children in Nursery to Year 4 also have classroom collections to use in addition to the school library. These classroom collections are selected by the teachers.

When choosing resources for this library it is important to remember that some of the children will have little access to any other library, and so the school library must provide resources for leisure interests as well as to support the curriculum. All materials are chosen with the diverse nature of the school community in mind, and to help give the children an awareness of the outside world. Efforts should also be made to reflect our increasingly diverse society.

The budget allocation for the library should be used to target any priority areas identified by the librarian in discussion with other staff before any other purchases are made. Reference should be made to the School Development Plan. Suggestions from other members of staff are always welcome.

Fiction

- This must be chosen to provide books for all the pupils in the school, catering for varying abilities and interests.
- Books should have up to date covers which look attractive.
- Recommendations made by the children should be considered carefully and may be bought, but it is for the librarian to make the final decision.
- Use is to be made of the School Library Service to supplement our own books, and also for the expertise of the SLS staff.
- The Red Spot Collection for Years 7 and 8 should contain books with a more mature

story line. (Some Year 6 pupils may borrow these books, but this is to be at the discretion of the librarian, the English teacher and possibly the pupil's parents.) Some adult stock may be bought for this, but it will be at the discretion of the librarian and the Head of English.
- Picture books will be bought for all ages.

Non Fiction

- This must be chosen to provide books for all the pupils in the school, catering for varying interests and abilities.
- Books should be up to date: especially in areas of frequent change such as science and technology.
- Recommendations from staff are to be sought to ensure that the stock reflects the needs of the curriculum.
- Recommendations made by the children should be considered carefully and may be bought, but it is for the librarian to make the final decision.

Audio

- These will be bought to supplement and complement the book stock.

Donations

- Donations are welcomed, but it is the decision of the librarian and other staff as to whether the item(s) should be added to stock.

Reviewing Magazines

The librarian should keep up to date with current book trends by use of reviews such as are included in *The School Librarian*, plus those from online review magazines such as *Books for Keeps* and various book-related websites, and by talking to other staff and children.

Author/Illustrator Visits

Books by visiting authors and illustrators should be purchased to satisfy interest following their visit.

Comments, Complaints and Concerns

Any parental concern about stock should be referred directly to the librarian.

Heather Bignold. Updated March 2016.

SLA **Guidelines:** Priority Paperwork

Reading For Pleasure

Our policy at Clayesmore Prep School

We believe that it is of the utmost importance that all our pupils are given the opportunity and the skills to develop their reading, in particular their reading for pleasure. This policy is for all staff at Clayesmore Prep School; teachers and support staff alike as we all have a role in encouraging our pupils to enjoy all forms of reading.

What is reading for pleasure?

We define reading for pleasure as pupils choosing some form of reading material themselves and then reading it primarily for enjoyment, often at times of their own choosing. We hope to create in our pupils a lifelong love of reading which will last long after they have left our school.

Why is it important?

There is an increasing amount of research showing that not only does reading for pleasure lead to an improvement in reading ability, it also can lead to a greater knowledge of other cultures, of general knowledge, of grammatical structures and spelling, and a greater awareness of others' emotional lives and journeys. It may even help our own emotional health and well-being. It is also shown to be one of the most important indicators of future economic success.

Choice of Reading Materials

We believe in a wide definition of **reading materials** which includes, but is not confined to:

- Picture books of varying levels of complexity for readers of all ages
- First readers
- Fiction of varying levels and degrees of complexity to suit pupils throughout the prep school
- Non fiction at various levels to support both the school curriculum and pupils' personal interests
- Audio books
- E-books (at present provided by the pupils themselves)
- Comics and magazines
- Newspapers
- Catalogues
- Specially selected books (both fiction and non-fiction) in more accessible formats.

The books, etc. in our school library are specially selected for our pupils, but reading materials can also be brought in from home.

It is vital that the library remains well stocked with new, varied and exciting titles in all categories in order for our pupils to be able to find things which will appeal to them. Being free to choose and being able to find something relevant is a very important part of encouraging reading for pleasure.

Access

We believe that it is important that pupils and staff have the fullest access to the library and so the prep school library is open throughout the school day, including before and after school, and at weekends. The library is staffed for 29 hours per week by a qualified, chartered librarian who can guide, support and encourage the pupils to develop their own tastes while exploring as widely as they wish.

Suggestions for creating readers

Book talk: One of the most important things anyone can do to encourage children and young people to read is to talk to them about books: what they are reading, what they like, what they don't like and also tell them what sort of things you enjoy reading. It is impossible to overestimate the influence of adults (and not just library and English staff) as reading role models for young people:

> "Librarians, teachers and children should spend time together just chatting about books, making recommendations to each other and generally sharing the joy of reading. It may seem a little informal, but the effect on reading would be remarkable, far greater than forced silent reading or writing book reviews. A good supply of high-quality books is essential, but no matter how extensive the resource collection, most important element of the 'conditions' to create readers is the presence of adults who are themselves readers – adults who read to pupils, talk about books and involve them in all sorts of literary activities"
> —Court (2011), p44.

Independent Reading: Allow time for personal reading when children can read to themselves a book they have chosen from the library or brought in from home.

Reading Aloud: Give time for reading to the children: sometimes this will be linked to the curriculum, but sometimes it should be for the sheer pleasure of sharing a book.

These things should exist alongside the more 'teaching' side of reading such as:

- Class readers
- Individual reading books
- Guided reading
- Developing literary skills in order to fully appreciate texts.

The importance of reading at home: Research shows that children, who come from families where reading is a valued activity and where adults read for pleasure, are much more likely to become frequent readers themselves. Thus, it is vital that as a school we foster links with parents and carers from the earliest possible stages and encourage them to enjoy sharing books with their children. Becoming a motivated, independent reader is not an overnight process, and our pupils need time, encouragement, lots of quality book choice and plenty of adult role models in order to make that transition.

Bibliography

- Court, Joy (2011). *Read to Succeed*. London: Facet. ISBN 9781856047470.

SLA **Guidelines:** Priority Paperwork

Appendix 4

Cambourne Village College, Cambridgeshire
Case Study, Library Policy and Development Plan

Alison Tarrant, Director of the SLA, previously school librarian at CVC. SLA School Librarian of the Year Honour List 2017.

Background

Cambourne Village College (VC) opened in 2013, a free school managed by the Cam Academy Trust, in Cambourne, Cambridgeshire. The new school was opened because the village was growing substantially, and the local council was transporting pupils 8 miles down the road to the nearest secondary school – Comberton Village College (also run by the Cam Academy Trust). As the population of Cambourne grew, transporting pupils became increasingly expensive for the council and demands were growing for there to be a secondary school within Cambourne.

In September 2013 Cambourne Village College opened with its first cohort of 143 Year 7 pupils and seven full time members of staff – while all other staff members split their time between Cambourne VC and Comberton VC. The school has been rapidly growing year on year, and in September 2017 our initial Year 7s are now our first Year 11s, and our current Year 7 cohort consists of 207 students. It was known when the school was initially opened that with the projected increases in local population that the school buildings would not be sufficient for more than a few years – they had been built to house 750 students, and yet it was projected that after five years we would need to accommodate 1,050 students – and so 2016/17 saw the school undergo a much needed building expansion. The pace of change in Cambourne is rapid and looks set to continue as a second campus is now planned – currently set to open in September 2019.

I was appointed in Easter 2013. I had been working as a Library Assistant in Comberton VC to gain experience in schools while completing the dissertation for my Library and Information Studies MSc Econ. and on completion of this was considering my next career step, when the Principal of Cambourne VC offered me the role as Librarian. This early appointment was really useful as it gave me a term without students to prepare for the opening of the brand new school library.

Why did I want the policies?

Some might think that given the never ending list of things that needs to be done when starting a library from scratch, that the 'paperwork' would be at the bottom of the list, but in reality I found the opposite to be true. The process of writing these was really important in thinking through the rationale, purpose and priorities of a school library, and how these were to going to be accomplished.

The policy was central to setting out what the library would look like, the research that backed that up, and what it would look like practically. This approach meant that it was a useful document – that I used to argue for funding, and to communicate to my colleagues, who had limited time on site, what they could expect from the library and use it for. Additionally, I gave a copy to the Governors so they too were aware of how the library was operating.

Having covered some youth librarianship issues during my Masters degree, and after working in a school library for several years I had a firm idea of the kind of library I wanted it to be, but this was also supported by my understanding of the needs of the future users. The catchment area of the new school was going to be different from that of Comberton VC. This mean that I would need to use different strategies for my new users who would present me with different opportunities and challenges.

I set about talking to the Head of English and the Principal to understand their thinking about the new library and if they shared my thoughts about the role the library might play in school life. Using the newly created policy as a starting point opened useful and constructive discussions about the aims and role of the library, and they were both supportive of the vision of a library service that I had created, and each contributed to my new Library Policy.

This important document was an opportunity to lay out my vision, the rationale and the practicalities of the library service that I wanted to run, and I had to convey this in brief to people who may have no knowledge of, or potentially even no interest in, the library. This is why the Mission Statement is so important – it lays out the essential themes of the policy in a few sentences, meaning that even if people get no further in their thinking or perhaps even their reading, they will know what the essence of the library is about.

Despite being reviewed on a yearly basis the Mission Statement has remained the same since 2013, while the sections about location, opening hours and staff have all changed as the school has developed and expanded.

The Facilities and Services sections have been tweaked over the years, but remain more or less the same, as does the Loan policy. However, the Code of Conduct has undergone a significant overhaul this year as the library extension has meant that the library can now seat just over 90 pupils, and in three different areas. This makes it harder for a single person, or even two, to maintain a constructive level of noise and purpose. We, as a school staff, have high expectations of behaviour, and the expectations for the library are no different – I am lucky to have unwavering support from the Senior Leadership Team (SLT) for this. However, having it form part of the policy means it is easier to train new staff (particularly duty staff), and should there be any complaints from parents I can show that I have acted in accordance with the agreed Library Policy.

When writing the policy, I felt it was important that I used it as an opportunity to lay out the expectations for the ongoing upkeep of the library, and also to demonstrate the research that supports the purpose of the library.

The Library policy was also a chance for me to be explicit about the Collection Policy – given that the school only had Year 7s, I was aware that the collection could be subject to scrutiny regarding the content of the books, so I wanted to make sure that I was protected to some degree, should there be a discussion or challenge to our book selection – fortunately this hasn't happened.

Starting a new school meant that we were all very aware that we would have an Ofsted inspection within the first two years. This meant that when that call came, I wanted to be in a strong position to demonstrate the value of the library, so having a process in place for being able to demonstrate this was important. To that end I wrote Termly Reviews, which were a more reflective and informal look at the ongoings of the term, while the Annual Report was a more formal examination of the feedback about the library. Essentially it was an examination of how the budget was spent and provided an opportunity to be explicit about the ways in which the library had helped the school meet its aims (more on this later). It was my intention to stop writing a Termly Review after the first few years, but actually I found they helped me achieve a sense of accomplishment as I looked back over the term, and appreciated the projects I had completed, the classes taught, assemblies delivered and books loaned, as well as making writing the Annual Report much easier. Having these built into the Annual Reports section means that people know what to ask for if they want more information about anything.

The evaluation section is central to the ethos of the library which builds into the ethos of the school itself. I also very much see myself as a research practitioner working in a profession that is sometimes hard pushed to produce 'data'. Evaluating practice helps me to assess whether something is worth the time/effort cost, and means that difficult decisions about how time is best spent can be taken on evidence rather than feeling.

The Liaison section was important because professional networking is essential: as well as being a cheap and effective way of continuing some elements of your professional development it is also important not to feel isolated as a loan practitioner especially when faced with the difficulties of maintaining a school library single-handedly. By including this in my policy document it gave me the necessary support and leverage should I be questioned about my reasons for attending a networking event, meeting or perhaps a local course.

Pupil Library Helpers are an essential part of my team – I am fortunate that I tend to attract large numbers of volunteers, and the library would not run as efficiently without them, and it is important this support and enthusiasm is recognised in the policy.

I believe that this policy was well constructed, and has only needed adjustment to reflect the changes that the school and library have gone through. It is sent to the governors, Principal and the member of SLT with responsibility for Line Management of the Librarian (currently the Assistant Principal (Curriculum) as it is updated.

In planning and creating this document, I was aware that there were challenges unique to Cambourne VC, particularly the low numbers of full-time staff, and starting a library with no pre-existing stock. It was exploring the issues that writing the policy exposed that meant we had a starting place for a development plan. Unlike the Library Policy, the Development Plan has existed in several different models over the five years since the library's inception, but I am confident that this is best version to date – it links directly with the school's development plan, which makes it significantly easier for everyone to understand how the library is contributing to the development of the school.

In the first year, there was so much to be done and knowing what my priorities should be was critical to the early success of the library. Having established these priorities in the development plan helped focus my mind, and enabled me to recognise that I was making progress, even with an ever growing to-do list! There's so much a library and librarian could potentially do, it was really important to have confidence that I was putting my energy and expertise into actions and strategies that were meaningful and useful, and actually helping to push the library forward in the ways that I and the school wanted.

The first page of the Library Development Plan is a mind map that lays out the priorities for the school development plan, and then the table is laid out in a similar manner to the school development plan. This is the template that all departments use – as much as the library sometimes falls between the Teaching/Support Staff chasm I think this is one area where the library fits into one category. There are a few items on the development plan that I put forward, but most are officially someone else's targets where the library can support and help achieve the aim.

Using this template means that I can easily keep track of what we've agreed to do, and the check points mean that we keep an eye on how we are progressing with these actions throughout the year. I normally dedicate a department meeting each half term to discussing the department development plan, putting plans in place, making specific times for completed and forthcoming actions, and discussing any obstacles and what we can do about them, in order to move forward. I use this development plan as a starting place for creating both my own and my library assistant's performance review targets – making sure that we are developing our skills and knowledge as the library needs, and that we are both becoming more competent and confident as time passes. Our Continuing Professional Development (CPD) is controlled by a member of SLT, and if we can prove that our CPD request links to our performance review and/or the development plan we are more likely to have the request agreed, so this process benefits everyone, as it keeps everything streamlined.

The Development Plan has been vital to making sure that the library developed in the most efficient and useful way, and I'm sure the Plan has been central to making SLT see the value of the library. The Annual Report at the end of each year demonstrates the key achievements of the library, and in order to be explicit about how they link with the school aims I put the number of the Development Plan aim at the end in brackets. This also streamlines the process so that the Principal, Governors or my Line Manager don't have to compare the two documents – they have everything they need in one place.

Doing policy and development plans do take a time commitment, but I am confident that my Library would not be as well placed without them. I have had a good budget, my staffing increased and my hours increased, and I couldn't have successfully argued for this without the evidence that the library was contributing towards driving the school forwards.

SLA **Guidelines:** Priority Paperwork

Library Policy

Reviewed 2017

Mission Statement

The Library supports independent and teacher-led learning and the discovery of material for pleasure. The Library works with all staff and departments, and is a key partner in cross curricular projects. The Library assists parents in supporting their children and works to ensure that pupils have a high level across all literacies.[17] The Library aims to work closely with libraries across the Cam Academy Trust.

Aims and Objectives

- Support the curriculum by stocking relevant, timely and up-to-date resources across a variety of formats.
- Support independent research by providing access to materials outside of lesson time.
- Encourage engagement by creating displays linking to current work, world events and literary subjects.
- Stock resources to support each pupil as a person including information on mental health, home and personal concerns and to assist with life decisions, such as careers and further education information.
- Research and trial new resources to help with studying and information literacy.
- Ensure that students and teaching staff are aware of, and adhere to, Anti-Plagiarism and Copyright codes of practice.
- Encourage reading for pleasure across all formats and types.
- Support reading across the curriculum by choosing relevant extracts and articles, and facilitating the recording of these.
- Support extension and intervention work across all departments to raise the levels of access.

Location and Opening Hours

The Library is located just off Reception, and is open from 8am until 4:30pm Monday, Wednesday and Thursday, and 8am to 4pm on Friday. On Tuesday it is open for 8am–4pm for all years, and on a trial basis from 4pm–5:30pm for Year 11 only. This will be reviewed on an ongoing basis throughout the year. If it is necessary to close for any reason pupils will be informed via tutors, the bulletin and posters around the school.

Library Staff

Cambourne Librarian – Ms Tarrant.
Library Assistant (part time: 32 hrs p/wk) – Mr Garcia-Fernandez.

---

[17] Reading, Writing and communication (Literacy) : Distance Learning materials for inspection within the new framework, OFSTED, October 2011, Version 4, p.10.

Duty staff are required at busy times to ensure that levels of behaviour remain high, and that the library is used in conjunction with its main purpose.

Facilities

The Library has one set of desks which seat up to 30 students. There is a research area of 18 computers and the information books, and there are an additional 9 computers in a separate area of the library. There are 10 iPads available to use as well. The Library can be booked out by any department, using either part or the whole space but multiple bookings will only be taken in exceptional circumstances. The Riddell Room can be booked separately, this seats up to 9 students.

Services

- Topic boxes for lessons
- Bookable space
- Computers
- Clickview
- Current Awareness provision
- Supporting the delivery of an Information Literacy programme
- Reader Advisory Service
- Assisting in the development of lesson plans and encouraging awareness of information literacy within subjects or schemes of work.

Loan Policy

- All pupils may borrow two fiction and two non-fiction items. Further borrowing is at the discretion of the library staff.
- All these items can be borrowed for 2 weeks initially, and can be renewed as necessary.
- All staff may borrow items for an initial period of one half-term unless requested by another borrower.
- A member of Library staff has to sign a leaver's notice to record that all items have been returned to the library.

Code of Conduct

- When in the library, pupils are required to abide by the school's Code of Conduct, ICT Acceptable Use policy, SAFE and PEOPLE codes and all other school codes.
- The library is a quiet working environment.
- Those pupils using the library outside of a class are to notify the library staff of their presence before using the facilities.
- Staff should email library staff in advance of sending their pupils, or send a note with them.
- In the case of poor behaviour the following processes and sanctions will apply:

- Immediate sanctions:
    - Being disruptive/not reading or working: – Warning
        – Asked to leave the library
    - Eating: – Asked to leave the library and a 40 min detention
    - Rudeness, arguing back or being purposefully disruptive: – Will result in being asked to leave the library, and a longer ban depending on severity of incident in conjunction with HoY/Deputy Principal
- Overdue Book Reminders – reminders are issued as a sticker in the diary
    - If reminders are ignored a letter will be sent home, in consultation with the Head of Year
    - If the book cannot be found a replacement or a contribution towards a new book will be charged. The contribution is fixed at £5 for a fiction book, and £10 for non-fiction.

Professional guidelines

We aim to adhere to School Library Association guidelines which stipulate that every secondary school library should provide:

- 13 items per pupil, of which 50% should be fiction, and 50% non-fiction
- A stock replenishment of 10% every year (after initial set up).

The average price of a paperback fiction title is £6.11, and the average price of a non-fiction hardback is £11.26.

The Chartered Institute of Library and Information Professionals recommend that there are 13 items per secondary school pupil.

Ofsted is aware of the difference that a good school library can make to a school:

'Libraries have always been central to education and self-improvement. They also have the power to act as motors for more dynamic and effective learning, whether for individuals or for groups. At school, college or university, the library plays a vital supportive role as a source of research and reading material or as a place of study.' [18]

In relation to the OFSTED standards, inspectors are told that: 'an attractive and well-stocked library is often an indicator of effective support for pupils' wider reading and information retrieval skills'[19] and the document goes on to highlight the importance of a librarian in encouraging pupils to read as well as ensuring pupils are reading at the right level and to provide guidance.

The report 'Good School Libraries: Making a Difference to Learning' highlighted that effective libraries are:

---

[18] *Empowering the learning community*, education and libraries task group, DfES, 2000.

[19] Reading, Writing and communication (Literacy) : Distance Learning materials for inspection within the new framework, OFSTED, October 2011, Version 4, p.35.

'…at the heart of pupils' learning [and] pupils enjoy access close to books and computers to support their work.' [20]

However, it also identified weaknesses in funding, accommodation, resources, management and staffing. In particular, it drew attention to missed opportunities to involve librarians in developing pupils' literacy.

It is useful to note that libraries are judged on the above criteria: funding, accommodation, resources, management and staffing. Another area that Ofsted have examined in the past is evaluation of the library. This will be dealt with below.

Collection Management

Selection – All books are chosen by the library staff in discussion with teachers where curriculum or subject knowledge is necessary. Fiction and non-fiction are equally important. We aim to supply books that pupils will enjoy, but there will also be stock that aims to challenge and extend their reading skills. The Library seeks to provide books that will enhance creative thinking, empathy, and a permanent love of books, as well as introducing students to new experiences. This means that books which may be deemed more challenging, either in content or style, are necessary. These will be given a content warning, however these are advisory only, and generally it is up to the children themselves to choose appropriate material. The Library staff will seek to read widely in order to appropriately classify material, but this is not always possible.

While the benefits of having resources that match the curriculum are obvious, there are many reports that highlight the importance of reading for pleasure:

- The National Literacy Trust found that reading for pleasure is the most important indicator of the future success of a child – http://www.literacytrust.org.uk/assets/0000/0402/Literacy_Changes_Lives_Executive_summary.pdf
- "Reading for pleasure is more important for children's educational success than their family's socio-economic status."   Organisation for Economic Co-operation and Development (OECD), Reading for Change, Programme for International Student Assessment (PISA)
- "A deep engagement with storytelling and great literature link directly to emotional development in primary children."   The Rose Review, 2008 Independent Review of the Primary School Curriculum
- "80% of children who read above the expected level for their age have books of their own; while only 58% who read below their expected level have books of their own." National Literacy Trust (NLT)
- "…research presents overwhelming evidence that literacy has a significant relationship with a person's happiness and success."   NLT

---

[20] Many libraries, especially in secondary schools, are more commonly known as 'learning resource centres'. Similarly, librarians are sometimes called 'learning resources managers'. This report uses the terms 'library' and 'librarian', except when quoting schools' own usage.

- "Leisure reading makes students more articulate, develops higher order reasoning, and promotes critical thinking." National Endowment for the Arts in To read or not to read, 2007
- "Children in England tend to report reading for pleasure less frequently than their peers in many other countries. There is a strong association between the amount of reading for pleasure children reported and their reading achievement." Progress in International Reading and Literacy Study (PIRLS); National Foundation for Educational Research, 2006, Twist et al. National Report for England

(taken from the Readathon website)

- "Teenagers who read in their spare time know 26% more words than those who never read" http://www.ucl.ac.uk/ioe/news-events/news-pub/nov-2017/reading-teenage-vocabulary; 2017
- "According to one source, if you read for twenty minutes a day you'll encounter an estimated 1,800,000 words over the course of a year whereas reading for only one minute a day will result in only 8,000 words." http://www.learningspy.co.uk/literacy/closing-language-gap-building-vocabulary/; 2014.

Weeding – Weeding will take place throughout the year, and decisions will be based on a variety of factors including: date of publication, wear, popularity, the number of copies held.

Donations – The library accepts donations gratefully, however, we maintain the right to use donations as we deem fit, and to redistribute any material that does not suit the needs of the pupils.

Annual Reports

The Library staff will produce the following annual reports to review progress and celebrate achievement over the year, as well as to provide direction and structure to the library. These will include a revision process of the Library Policy, a Library Development Plan, and an Annual Review, which will provide an informal look into the achievements of the library.

Library Policy – sets out the general rules and terms of use of the library. This will enable all staff to see where the library may be of use to them, and give the Library a clear mission statement and aim. This will be reviewed yearly and updated when necessary.

Library Development Plan – looks ahead over 3–5 years, and laying out important action that needs to be taken in order for the library to maintain a high quality service. It will identify potential weaknesses and how they can be managed. Areas for development will link into the development plan of the school.

Annual Review – documents the progress, events, competitions and achievements of the library each year. This may be supplemented by reflections written at the end of each term.

Evaluation

Ofsted have highlighted the importance of evaluation as a tool to improve the library, making it the first recommendation in their 'Good School Libraries: Making a Difference to Learning' Report. Reflection on the service provided by the Library will be sought from staff, pupils and parents. The opinions of each stakeholder will be gathered through surveys, focus groups and on a one to one informal basis.

Evaluation into the impact of the range of activities that we do will also be carried out, some of which may be taken further and extended into a research project, and written up to share with colleagues, which builds into the school's ethos as a research school.

Liaison with External Organisations

The Library will develop relationships with external organisations to provide a comprehensive and reflexive service. These organisations include: Cambridgeshire Public Library Service, local bookshops, publishers and charities such as the National Literacy Trust, Booktrust as well as professional organisations such as the Chartered Institute of Library and Information Professionals, the Youth Libraries Group and the School Library Association. Additionally, networking with school librarians from across Cambridgeshire and beyond is key to personal development and sharing best practice.

Library volunteers – The Library runs a Pupil Library helpers scheme which helps pupils gain leadership experience and gain their pink pin badges. Interested pupils can apply in the Autumn term, to start soon after. The scheme runs in all Years, with the pupils being involved in helping with the day to day running of the library, assisting with events, and having a say on how the Library is run, and choosing stock. Various positions of special responsibility will be created and managed as necessary.

Links to other policies or protocols

- Plagiarism
- Copyright
- School's Code of Conduct
- ICT Acceptable Use policy.

References

Lighthouse Professional Development, "Steps to Success in Managing an Outstanding LRC"

Barrett, L. and J. Douglas, eds. "The CILIP guidelines for secondary school libraries", CILIP, 2004

CILIP, DoE, SLA and ASCEL. "School Libraries: Making a Difference" (n.d.)

http://www.sla.org.uk/advice-book-stock.php

http://www.sla.org.uk/advice-spending-levels.php

OFSTED, "Good School Libraries: Making a difference to learning" (2006)

OFSTED, Reading, Writing and communication (literacy) : Distance learning materials for inspection within the new framework, October 2011, Version 4.

If you are interested in the professional guidelines that are set out, we have many books and booklets on the subject in the library office.

Created May 2013. Revised Sep 2017.

SLA Guidelines: Priority Paperwork

Camborne Village College Library Development Plan

Departmental strategic intent	Action	Success criteria	Timescale; individual/s responsible	Progress at Feb half term	Development, training, research, support, resources needed	Relation to School Development Plan
Excellent attainment by Year 11 pupils in external exams.	Promote and evaluate the late night openings. Adjust with demand.	Late night openings are attended by 30% of Year 11; particularly those identified as requiring additional support.	Dec 17 Mar 18 Jul 18 AT	Attendance on Tuesday (ave 13/14) is higher than other days, but only 9% of year group. However, attendees are mostly PP/have restricted facilities at home.	Time	1.2 To ensure Year 11 pupils consolidate and accelerate their expected and exceeding- expected progress levels
Strong and genuine progress made at KS3.	Ensure adequate support for all topics, including on Clickview and Reading Lists.	90% of KS3 teachers feel library supports their teaching.	Dec 17 Jul 18 FG/AT	Will be built into staff survey.	Time	1.1 To ensure that the proportions of pupils matching and exceeding expected progress in Years 7, 8 and 9 are in line with, or above those for 2016/17
Ensure all subjects have embedded reading across Year 9 Scheme of Works by the end of the year, and all texts are available as audio files.	Support, cajole and encourage all teachers to embed the reading and make sure it is used.	For 100% of departments to have readings for Year 9 SoW and for analysis of SMHW to show that reading homeworks have been set.	Nov 17 Dec 18 Apr 18 AT	EM updated as to progress – most of Year 9 departments done, with a few outstanding.	Time	2.1 To embed high-quality reading materials, in a meaningful way, across the curriculum, to develop vocabulary and to secure and enhance subject understanding.
Staff survey to show that teachers are aware of and use Research Process. Support all staff in implementation where necessary.	Deploy staff survey, support schemes of work and co-teaching of lessons.	For 80% of departments to be using research process within at least one scheme of work.	Nov 17 Jan 18 Mar 18 AT	Will be built into staff survey.	Time	2.2 To develop the Information Literacy initiative and to evaluate outcomes.

SLA Guidelines: Priority Paperwork

Develop links with IES 'EL Convento' in Bornos in Cadiz.	Ensure that relationship with Spanish school is built, and is viable	For students to be engaging with Spanish school via Twitter and Blogs	Nov 17 Mar 18 Jul 18 FG	Communication is happening via Twitter. Video reviews, recommendations and opinion exchanges are happening – CamVC pupils are doing this in Spanish.	Time	2.3 To develop further opportunities for international links and visits and to write these into the curriculum, especially to support the teaching of Spanish.
Make sure that knowledge and best practice are disseminated across the Trust	Maintain email contact and one meeting yearly.	For meeting/emails to be useful both ways		Ongoing.		4.2 To develop opportunities to share best practice in teaching and learning across the Trust
Support Lead Practitioner Programme	AT applies to takes part in LP	For AT to successfully be accepted onto LP programme, accredited LP and to evaluate programme	Dec 17 Jul 18 AT	AT withdrew, allowing place to be given to someone else.	Time	4.4 To introduce the Lead Practitioner initiative, developing the role of the LP in leading teaching and learning initiatives, CPL and research.
Support reading for pleasure in primaries – supporting reading communities and teaching of reading.	AT to attend CB23 meetings, events for primaries, produce reading grids for primaries and run a 'Teachers as Readers' group	Attitude to Reading surveys show an increase in positive attitudes towards reading, and all primaries involved in events.	Dec 17 Mar 18 Jul 18 AT	AT running Teachers as Readers group – 3 primary teachers attending atm. Author event booked in for WBD week – Friday 2nd March.	Time	4.8 To strengthen links with Jeavons Wood Primary school, and seek ways to extend this cooperation to other catchment primary schools.
Support the pilot of IT programme, by being able to support teachers and pupils use of relevant IT	FG to do training on iPads, either through Apple or other relevant body.	FG has completed training	Dec 17 Mar 18 Jul 18 FG	FG has been given iPad, now in early stages of implementing and exploring opportunities for iPad use in library lessons. Working with some English teachers to plan content.	Time/ money	4.10 To review the place of IT in teaching and learning, including the implementation of the BYO device initiative for pupils.
Support development of teaching school	AT to offer to run course through teaching school	Progress has been made on whether this is viable and useful; course is planned and ready to be delivered in September	Dec 17 Mar 18 Jul 18 AT	On hold.	Time/ others time	4.12 To develop the role of the Teaching School
Library runs a session as part of Induction. All staff receive a 'Library Guide'	AT makes sure JJ has 'Library Guides' and plans for NQT session to run for all new staff next year.	All New staff are aware of library offers	Dec 17 Mar 18 Jul 18 AT	Some bags left over from beginning of the year. To be given out to staff as they arrive.	Time/ others	4.14 To develop and implement a full programme of induction for new teaching staff.

SLA Guidelines: Priority Paperwork

Library conducts research as part of ongoing evaluation, and disseminates this.	AT completes CTSN course, and LP project. FG continues to work on MSc Dissertation	AT completes both courses; FG is confident in dissertation and has resources he needs	Dec 17 Mar 18 Jul 18 AT/FG	AT dropped out of both courses. FG is making good progress on dissertation – modules are now completed, allowing full focus on dissertation. Needs to be completed by 1/10/2018.	Time/Data	4.15 To enhance the position of research at CamVC by embedding the role of Research Coordinator.
Clickview is regularly used across all departments. Situation with Comberton Clickview is resolved.	AT sends regular updates to staff and offers training. FG has regular slot to update programmes	80% of staff using Clickview and 50% of pupils in KS4 using Clickview.	Dec 17 Mar 18 Jul 18 AT/FG	Will be built into survey. There have been 1500 video views in the last 180 days, there have been 1246 logins – 89% by staff. It is being used at ComVC as well as CamVC.	Time	4.18 To evaluate the use of Clickview and to plan for its future development
All Library information is up to date and clear, with correct links	AT checks pages and keeps ST informed of any changes.	All Library information is up to date.	Dec 17 Mar 18 Jul 18 AT	Needs checking – some links have been updated – there isn't anything overtly out of date, but will need changing when DB starts.	Time	4.20 To ensure that all information on the College website is current and relevant.
Ensure link governor is up to date with all information required	AT to have 2 meetings yearly with RH	Link governor is confident in output of school library.	Dec 17 Mar 18 Jul 18 AT	Governors informed of AT departure, and DB appointment.	Time	4.29 To enhance governance further by consolidating the roles of link governors.

Appendix 5 Corby Business Academy Library Development Plan

Amy McKay, Librarian. SLA Board member 2017–20 and SLA School Librarian of the Year 2016.

Corby Business Academy is a popular high achieving non-selective coeducational secondary school in Corby, Northamptonshire, for students aged 11–18.

Department: Library				
Priority: Engagement				
Action	Staff	Date / Timescale	Success Criteria	Progress
To offer a varied Session 4 programme that appeals to different student interests. This will include regular provision for the library to remain as an area for quiet study, whilst also offering a range of activities. Activities will include Lego Club, Corby Book Addicts, Manga focuses, author visits and trips off site.	AMMK CHMA	All year	Library has been well used during Session 4, with a range of activities having been offered. Participation % have increased 5% on last year's %.	T1 T2 T3 T4 T5 T6
What the library looks like profiles for EAL, SEN, Boys, FSM created. Considering how the library meets the needs to all users.	AMMK	Jan	Profiles created. Results considered and acted upon where necessary. If it is found that a particular group are not having their needs met then interventions and focused activities will be introduced.	T1 T2 T3 T4 T5 T6

SLA Guidelines: Priority Paperwork

Action	Responsible	Timing	Success Criteria					
				T2	T3	T4	T5	T6
The library will continue to encourage the development of intellectual curiosity by stocking and promoting appealing and high-quality fiction and non-fiction books.	AMMK CHMA	All year	Borrowing and usage figures. Range of stock added to catalogue. Borrowing figures have increased. % figures used to show recent purchases are well borrowed.					
Reader development activities will be offered to encourage development.		All year	Take up of a range of reader development activities. % figures to show number of students participating in activities.					
Promotion of non-fiction will be increased and focused upon to ensure students are aware of the opportunities to read around their subjects. Book display boxes will be trialled in the library to raise awareness of high-interest non-fiction.		December onwards	Increase in non-fiction use. Non-fiction borrowing figures have increased 10% compared to 2012-13.					

Action	Responsible	Timing	Success Criteria	T1	T2	T3	T4	T5	T6
Target reader development at non-traditional library users. Offer tutor time sessions to KS3 reluctant readers (in conjunction with tutors).	AMMK CHMA	Nov onwards	Tutor time sessions have been attended and attitudes and borrowing of reluctant readers to be improving. At least 50% of reluctant readers will show an improvement in attitude and will become regular library users.						

SLA Guidelines: Priority Paperwork

Priority: Classroom Practice

Action	Staff	Date / Timescale	Success Criteria	Progress
Induction programme to continue as is. Inductions offered for Y7s, Y12s and staff. Non-attending staff and Y12s pursued and rebooked in. Extension activities offered for Y7s.	AMMK	Sept	Inductions complete. 90% take up for staff and students. 25% of Y7s participate in extension activities.	T1
				T2
				T3
				T4
				T5
				T6
				T1
				T2
				T3
				T4
				T5
				T6
				T1
				T2
				T3
				T4
				T5
				T6

SLA Guidelines: Priority Paperwork

Priority: Curriculum Development				
Action	Staff	Date / Timescale	Success Criteria	Progress
Develop range of stock to ensure it is relevant and addresses changes to curriculum, particularly for KS5.	AMMK CHMA	Ongoing	Relevant stock available and being used. 90% of new stock regularly borrowed.	T1
				T2
				T3
				T4
				T5
Research and invest in online resources for the A-Level curriculum.		Nov 2013	Online resources purchased and promoted to staff and students.	T6
Promotion of 'reading across the curriculum' booklists to all DoS, develop new lists as required. Publicise lists on VLE.	AMMK CHMA	Ongoing	VLE access organised	T1
			Booklists publicised.	T2
			DoS aware of booklists – 20% of booklists used by staff to promote wider reading.	T3
				T4
				T5
				T6
Target CKG shadowing at most able students, write to parents explaining scheme using OU research. Invite GandT students to a library launch of longlist. Establish online and tutor time groups in addition to S4 that will offer all students the opportunity to shadow	AMMK CAMA	Feb onwards	Shadowing take up increased amongst most able students. 50% of targeted most able students have shadowed at least one shortlisted book.	T1
				T2
				T3
				T4
				T5
				T6

SLA Guidelines: Priority Paperwork

Priority: Progress

Action	Staff	Date / Timescale	Success Criteria	Progress
Get a list of pupil premium students/FSM/LAC, look out how many of them are regular library users. Target those that aren't for reader development activities.	AMMK CHMA	Nov onwards	List secured and considered. Students targeted. Increase in participation of pupil premium students.	T1
				T2
				T3
				T4
				T5
				T6
Continue to monitor borrowing gap between boys and girls. React accordingly to any changes in balance.	AMMK CHMA	Ongoing	Borrowing gap has closed.	T1
				T2
				T3
				T4
				T5
				T6
				T1
				T2
				T3
				T4
				T5
				T6

SLA Guidelines: Priority Paperwork

Appendix 6

Ripon Grammar School
Library Policy and Development Plan

Sally Dring is the Librarian and Literacy and Numeracy Coordinator at the school. She is also Chair of the Yorkshire and Humberside branch of the SLA and a member of the SLA Board.

Ripon Grammar School is an outstanding, high achieving, selective co-educational state grammar school with boarding facilities of approximately 900 students.

Library Policy

Mission Statement

The School Library supports Ripon Grammar School in its aim to create a stimulating, caring and rewarding school environment where every student is valued and supported to ensure they fulfill their potential, where they are happy and where they feel encouraged to achieve.

Aims & Objectives:

- To support teaching and learning within the school to enable students to achieve the highest academic standards possible.
- To promote reading for pleasure and fostering a genuine love for reading.
- To educate students about research skills, referencing, information literacy and academic honesty.
- To provide a rich and wide range of resources in a variety of media formats, including access to resources at different locations such as the British Library.
- To promote literacy and numeracy skills.
- To organise resources to allow easy retrieval.
- To encourage staff and students to see the Library as a learning space and a warm, welcoming environment.
- To ensure that all 1st Year students receive formal Library lessons on a weekly basis.

Management of the Library and Learning Centre

- The School Librarian will have overall responsibility for the management and administration of the Library and Learning Centre.
- The School Librarian and Library Assistant will have responsibility for the day to day management and running of the Library and Learning Centre.
- To provide for continuing professional development, Library staff may be released when necessary for in-service training or general professional development – e.g. training courses, professional body meetings, etc.

- Pupil Librarians are recruited from 2nd year upwards on a voluntary basis. A rota is in place so Pupil Librarians are aware which break time and lunch time they are on duty. Their role is to re-shelve, tidy their area and loan/return books. If a Pupil Librarian is not on duty then they are not to be behind the desk.

Accommodation

Library

- The Library has IT facilities which include an IT room (12 PCs), a gallery area (14 PCs) and a laptop trolley (15 laptops).
- It can seat up to 40 students at study tables downstairs, with access for disabled students.
- The Library has a comfy reading area with bean bags and chairs for students.
- The gallery is a Sixth Form only area unless booked for lessons. Sixth Form students are not permitted to use the gallery if the Library is booked for a lesson unless otherwise agreed with either the teacher or Librarian/Library Assistant.

Learning Centre

- The Learning Centre can seat up to 40 students at study tables, with access for disabled students.
- 15 Laptops are available from a laptop trolley.
- The Learning Centre also contains a 'Careers' room which is used in conjunction with the Careers department.
- There are sofas and bean bags for students to relax and read or do work on.
- The Learning Centre is stocked with non-fiction books, textbooks and subject specific wider reading, as well as fiction for reading for pleasure.

Careers

- The Careers department is situated within the Library at the top of the stairs. Students can drop in or make an appointment. Appointments are available with the current Career department member of staff or with an independent careers adviser.
- There are regular Career workshops for students where experts from particular areas of experience give talks in school.

Green Room

- The Green Room is situated within the Library at the top of the stairs. It is manned and supervised by the Inclusion Team and is not available for general use.

Resources

- Subject specific materials will be selected by the Librarian and Library Assistant after consultation with Heads of Departments and teaching staff.
- General reading material will be selected by the School Librarian and Library Assistant and will take into account requests from staff and students.

SLA Guidelines: Priority Paperwork

- Equipment will be audited by the Librarian/Library Assistant on an annual basis to ensure that it is safe and suitable.
- Resources will be audited by the Librarian/Library Assistant on a biennial basis to ensure that it is up to date and relevant.
- The stock should be well maintained and displayed to promote its use.
- Stock will be regularly edited to remove out of date, unsuitable or unattractive items using the recommended guidelines (School Library Association).
- The Library should be stocked with an adequate number of up to date, attractive and relevant resources to support the curriculum and leisure needs of staff and students, in line with recommended stocking levels (School Library Association).
- The Library is equipped with a colour printer/photocopier and a black and white printer/photocopier. $1^{st} - 5^{th}$ years need to ask a teacher/Librarian or Library Assistant for help with photocopying. Each Sixth Form student has their own photocopying code and needs to collect this from the Sani.
- Staff are asked to refrain from sending students down with large amounts of photocopying unless they have provided the student with their department code.

Use of resources

- The Library management system is Oliver, a database for all resources and loans.
- All staff and students will be enrolled in Oliver and may borrow as follows:

	No of items	Loan period
$1^{st} - 5^{th}$ years	3	2 weeks
6th Form	10	3 weeks
Staff	20	6 months

- Renewals can be made.
- Overdue letters will be sent twice every half-term via form tutors. If items are over 100 days overdue, email invoices will be sent home to parents. A replacement charge may be made for non-returned/lost items.

Usage

- The Librarian and Library Assistant reserve the right to refuse to photocopy material if it is in breach of copyright legislation.
- Staff are encouraged to book the Library for lessons requiring group work and research.
- Students are able to use the Library during form time and registration as long as they have permission from their form tutors.
- Form tutors are encouraged to book the Library during form time for sessions – most year groups have a session every term in the Library during form time.
- The Learning Centre is specifically for the use of Sixth Form unless otherwise agreed with the Sixth Form team – this is a silent working area only.
- The Library may be used by the Sixth Form during their free periods, but priority is given to teaching staff who book the Library.

SLA **Guidelines:** Priority Paperwork

- The Library can be used as a space for students to catch up with their work during lesson time if permission has been given by their teacher.
- The Library should not be used as a 'dumping ground' for badly behaved students.
- Students sent to work/research in the Library during lesson times should have a note from their teacher giving them permission to do so.

Future Developments

The Library aims:
- To continue to develop the positive relationships with other departments
- To continue encouraging students to use the Library for work or pleasure through their own personal choice
- To develop a curriculum map so the Library is aware of what topics are being taught during the academic year and which resources are required for this
- To further promote the Library as a safe space for students to support their mental well-being.

Responsibility of SLT and teachers towards the Library:

- Departments will be requested to keep the Library informed on curriculum changes so that appropriate resources can be maintained.
- All staff should encourage students to use the Library but to be respectful and follow the School's rules regarding behaviour and conduct.

Behaviour/Rules – Library:

- No bags in the Library – they must either be in the cloakroom or on the shelves provided outside the Library – <u>NOT on the floor</u>.
- No food or drink except for bottled water.
- Students must be using the Library either to read or do work and not as a general common room.
- Students must follow the lunch time rota system when it is in place.
- When the Library is booked for a lesson, students must not use the Library unless otherwise agreed with the Librarian or Library Assistant.
- Noise level should not be too loud.
- Language should be appropriate for school.
- NO mobile phones allowed unless otherwise agreed with the Librarian or Library Assistant.
- The Gallery is for Sixth Form only unless otherwise agreed with the Librarian/Library Assistant.
- If students want to use the Library during form time or registration they need to have prior permission from their form tutor.
- If the Library is booked for a lesson then only the students in that lesson may use the Library/Gallery unless otherwise agreed with the teacher or Library/Library Assistant.

SLA **Guidelines:** Priority Paperwork

Behaviour/Rules – Learning Centre

- Bags are to be placed in the cubby holes provided.
- No food or drink allowed except for bottled water.
- Silent working only.
- Phones should only be used for listening to music or research – not for social media or texting. If there is any doubt over mobile phone usage during school hours please refer to the school mobile phone policy.
- Students should not be in the Learning Centre before period 1 unless permission has been given.

The Librarian/Library Assistant hold the right to restrict access to students who do not follow the rules of the Library.

Opening Hours

Library
Monday – Thursday: 8:30am – 5:00pm
Friday: 8:30am – 4:00pm

Learning Centre
Monday – Friday: 9:15am – 4:00pm

Opening times may vary if Library staff are unavailable at certain times or the Library is being used for events.

Development Plan

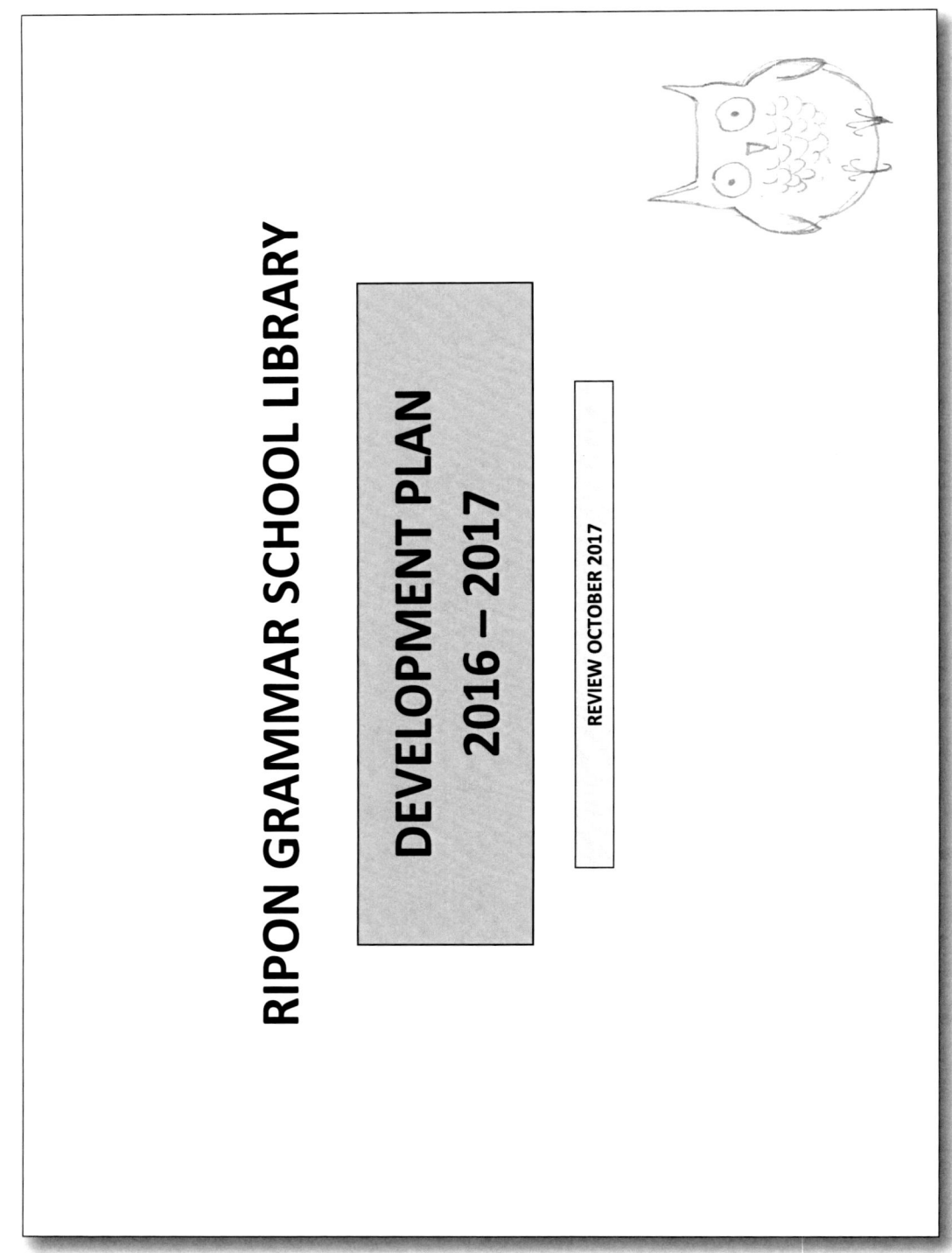

AREA	RGS TARGET	LIBRARY TARGET	ACTION	UPDATE OCTOBER 2017
TEACHING LEARNING & CURRICULUM		Ensure the best and most relevant resources are available	Serious overhaul of library resources. Many books, particularly textbooks, are out of date and underused. Refine print stock and improve digital stock	Overhaul has begun with many old books withdrawn and discussions with subject departments. LH liaising with departments.
	TLC1 Maximise attainment (including vulnerable groups)	Focus on generic skills such as 'grit', focus, proofreading, etc.	Adapt Success Builder to include these skills and promote.	Generic skills discussed in the T&L sessions led by SD and amendments to Success Builder made. Group members are auditing response. Decided to go ahead and there is now a monthly Success Builder displayed around school.
		Raise awareness of plagiarism and its consequences	• Increase involvement with year groups, particularly sixth form. • Develop a whole school Academic Honesty Policy.	• Limited access to 6th Form. Short Form Time L6 induction which didn't allow time for this. • Academic Honesty Policy developed by LH Has gone to Governors – awaiting response.
	TLC4 L & N across the curriculum		SEE LITERACY & NUMERACY ACTION PLAN	
	TLC8 Induction of first years -	Assist SENCO in working with new 1st form students to embed expectations and 'soft' skills	Improve Library Lesson curriculum to target these skills. Work with departments to promote these skills across the curriculum	Working closely with SENCO to promote organisation, presentation, etc. Seems to be going well during library lessons – Need to discuss with teaching staff to see if any improvement on previous years.
STAFF DEVELOPMENT	ST1 Develop staff expertise through effective CPD	CPD for new Library Assistant	• LH begins 2 year masters course in Information and library management through Northumbria University • SD continues with training, focussing on confidence to deliver sessions • LH becomes member of CILIP (Chartered Institute of Library & Information Professionals)	• LH passed first year and has started work on the second year of her Masters course • Confidence now growing fast and LH has delivered both form time sessions, as well as sessions to visiting primary pupils. • LH now member of CILIP
		Remain aware of the wider professional body	Continue as mentor for 3 librarians working towards Chartership.	Ongoing, but one has moved to Scotland and another has been ill.
		Develop an Academic Honesty Policy	Attend training course in York on 'The Copy & Paste Generation'	Course was cancelled due to lack of interest. Policy developed in-house.

SLA Guidelines: Priority Paperwork

AREA	RGS TARGET	LIBRARY TARGET	ACTION	UPDATE OCTOBER 2017
PASTORAL	PA2 PSHCEe curriculum development	Bank of resources to support	Work closely with new PSHCEe co-ordinator to ensure excellent support is given	Informal discussions taking place and resources for projects building up. Joint project introduced in Summer Term – development of research and information literacy skills along with discovery of generic skills needed to succeed.
COMMUNITY	COM1 Stronger links with parents and alumni	Provide resources for parents	Develop a bank of resources for the school website	Summer term. Reading challenge for parents and students?? Reading challenge publicised on website and in library, but no response
	COM3 Links with primary schools strengthened	Links with primary schools strengthened	Deliver literacy sessions to Y6 pupils as part of the STEM project and try to build on this.	Very successful series of literacy sessions delivered to Y6 students – excellent feedback. Further sessions have taken place with Y5 during Autumn 2017. Again very successful. Attempt to link in with primary curriculum.
FACILITIES & RESOURCES	FR2 Strategic plan for effective, costed and affordable on-going maintenance	Refresh library environment	Table tops re-surfaced	Table tops were resurfaced during Easter 2017. Looking cleaner but not as tough.
			Freshen paintwork	Further improvements on hold for financial reasons.
			Library re-design – organise quotes	

SCD October 2017

Bibliography

ALL PARTY PARLIAMENTARY GROUP FOR LIBRARIES (2014) *The Beating Heart of the School: Improving educational attainment through school libraries and librarians.* Viewed at https://www.cilip.org.uk/sites/default/files/documents/BeatingHeartoftheSchool.pdf [accessed 2/10/17]

CILIP *Existing Ethical Framework* (revised 2012) https://www.cilip.org.uk/research/topics/ethics-review/existing-ethical-framework [accessed 19/10/17]

CILIP INFORMATION LITERACY GROUP website https://infolit.org.uk/

DEPARTMENT FOR EDUCATION AND SKILLS (2004) *Improve your Library: a Self-Evaluation Process for Primary Schools.* DfES. Viewed at http://dera.ioe.ac.uk/5293/1/Self-evaluation%20process%20for%20Primary%20school%20libraries.pdf [accessed 3/10/17]

DEPARTMENT FOR EDUCATION AND SKILLS (2004) *Improve your library: a self-evaluation process for secondary school libraries and learning resource centres.* DfES. Viewed at https://101tips.files.wordpress.com/2008/01/self-evaluation-process-for-secondary-school-libraries-and-lrcs.pdf [accessed 10/11/17]

DEPARTMENT FOR EDUCATION (2014) *National Curriculum in England: English programmes of study.* Viewed at https://www.gov.uk/government/publications/national-curriculum-in-england-english-programmes-of-study/national-curriculum-in-england-english-programmes-of-study [accessed 3/10/17]

DUNCAN, SALLY (2010) *Making a Start with your Primary School Library.* School Library Association

GREENWOOD, HELEN, CREASER, CLAIRE and MAYNARD, SALLY (2008) *Successful Primary School Libraries: Case studies of good practice.* Booktrust. Viewed at http://www.lboro.ac.uk/microsites/infosci/lisu/downloads/successful-prim-sch-libs.pdf [accessed 3/10/17)

INTERNATIONAL FEDERATION OF LIBRARY ASSOCIATIONS AND INSTITUTIONS (2015) IFLA *School Library Guidelines.* Viewed at https://www.ifla.org/files/assets/school-libraries-resource-centers/publications/ifla-school-library-guidelines.pdf [accessed 2/10/17]

SCHOOL LIBRARY ASSOCIATION website http://www.sla.org.uk/index.php

SCOTTISH LIBRARY AND INFORMATION COUNCIL (2017) *How Good is Our School Library?* SLIC. Viewed at http://scottishlibraries.org/media/1665/hgiosls-pdf.pdf [accessed 4/10/17]

TAYLOR, LAURA (2018) *New Beginnings: A Practical Guide to Taking Charge of a Secondary School Library.* School Library Association.

TERAVAINEN, ANNE and CLARK, CHRISTINA (2017) *School Libraries: A literature review of current provision and evidence of impact.* National Literacy Trust. https://literacytrust.org.uk/research-services/research-reports/school-libraries-literature-review-current-provision-and-evidence-impact-2017/ [accessed 3/10/17]

Also available from the SLA

Historical Fiction for the School Library: Riveting Reads
by Dawn Finch

978-1-911222-18-7   £15.00 (SLA members £11.00)

If you're looking for some 'Riveting Reads' in the genre of historical fiction, then this guide is perfect for your requirements. Written by author and librarian Dawn Finch, with a foreword by SLA Patron and former President Kevin Crossley-Holland, this publication provides a strong introduction to what a historical novel is, why children should be encouraged to read historical fiction, and also some important tips for choosing historical fiction.

Historical Fiction for the School Library offers a superb selection of concise book reviews covering Pre-History, Ancient Greece, Egyptians, Romans, and the period from the 5th Century AD to the World Wars – encompassing text and picture books. It also includes references to poetry, anthologies and series books.

Chaos or Collection?: Selecting and Managing Graphic Novels in Your School Library
by Neena Morris

978-1-911222-12-5   £13.50 (SLA members £9.00)

Graphic novels are some of the most exciting and varied resources that school librarians have on their shelves, and they are growing ever more popular with all kinds of readers. But knowing how to select, catalogue, classify and shelve them so your library users can find them can be challenging. Here Neena Morris, one of the librarians at Ardingly College in West Sussex, tells us what she does to maintain an exciting and eclectic collection that is easily identified, managed effectively, accessible to all and widely enjoyed by her students. Building on the research that she conducted for her Masters degree, this how-to guide is very readable and full of common sense suggestions – there are lessons here for all of us.

Cultivating Curiosity: Information Literacy Skills and the Primary School Library
by Geoff Dubber and Sarah Pavey

978-1-911222-15-6   £13.50 (SLA members £9.00)

Cultivating curiosity in children in primary schools is one of the most important things that we can do for them. Developing an enthusiasm for learning is at the very heart of human development and a central reason for teaching information and digital literacy, and is a crucial focus for school library work. This new edition includes information about the most recent primary curriculum, government initiatives and recent inspection changes in respect of the school library and digital media. It explains the importance of embedding information literacy into a whole school and curriculum context, making use of modern technology where appropriate. It outlines and explains the processes of research for young children and shows ways that teachers and librarians can develop and promote information and digital literacy through the primary school library and link it to classroom practice. It also includes a very useful and practical case study, some templates and a reading list.